From Stutter to Strategy.

The Making of a Māori Tech Founder.

Contents

ISBN: [Leave blank if using Amazon's free ISBN]

First published in 2026

Printed in the United Kingdom

Author contact:

Jay Skipworth

Dedication

This book is dedicated to:

My Wife Silvia.
My rock, my grounding force,
my inspiration,
my future.
Your presence brings balance.
Your belief brings strength.
Your love brings light into every chapter of my life.

To my loving family.
Who carry my heart, my history and my hope.
Kia kaha i roto i te ora e tōku whānau.
(Stand strong in this life, my family).
Your support, your laughter and your loyalty
have carried me further than words can ever express.

And to my *paua* (abalone) Rhea, our German Shepherd
my loyal companion, protector, and calm presence on the hardest
days.
You remind me that love comes in many forms
and that loyalty is sometimes spoken without a single word.

This book is for all of you.

Preface

This book was never meant to present a perfect life, a clean arc, or a story that resolves itself neatly at the final page. It was never written to offer easy answers or to suggest that growth follows a straight line. What lives in these chapters is something far more honest than that. This is a human story. One shaped by struggle and resilience, by identity and loss, by failure and rebuilding, and by the quiet victories that rarely receive applause but change us forever.

The moments that mattered most in my life did not arrive with recognition or validation. They arrived quietly. In solitude. In reflection. In the decision to keep moving when stopping would have felt safer. Many of the turning points you will read about happened far from the spotlight, in places where no one was watching, where the only witness was the person I was becoming.

I did not write this book as someone who has everything figured out. I wrote it as someone who has had to learn, again and again, how to stand back up. Someone who carried doubt longer than he wanted to admit. Someone who felt fear, uncertainty, and the heavy weight of responsibility settle on his shoulders at different stages of life. This book exists not because hardship was avoided, but because it was endured. And because even when the path ahead felt unclear, I chose to continue forward rather than turn back.

My life has taken me through many rivers, each demanding something different from me. There were the uncertain waters of childhood, where identity begins to form before you have the language to describe it. Where confidence and vulnerability live side by side. There were the deep currents of grief that arrived with the loss of my parents, losses that reshape not just the heart, but how you see the world and your place within it. There were the internal battles with my own voice, learning not only how to speak clearly, but how to speak without fear. How to trust that my words, even when they arrived slowly, still mattered.

There were mistakes that humbled me. Moments where pride gave way to perspective. Lessons that did not arrive gently, but stayed because they were earned the hard way. There were relationships that taught me patience, tenderness, and humility. And there was the journey of fatherhood, a role that grounded me, stretched me, and taught me responsibility in its truest form. Becoming a parent reshaped my understanding of success, reminding me that the most meaningful work we do is often unseen.

Later in life came a spark I did not expect. A pull toward entrepreneurship, technology, and the rapidly evolving world of artificial intelligence, long after many people assume such chapters are closed. It would have been easy to accept that belief. To tell myself that reinvention belonged to younger minds, to people with fewer scars and more time ahead of them. Instead, I chose curiosity over comfort. Courage over certainty. And that choice changed everything.

I stand in this story as a Māori (Indigenous people of New Zealand) man shaped by the strength of my ancestry. By the resilience of Ngāti Porou (tribe from the East Coast of New Zealand). By the determination and fire of Ngā Puhi (tribe from Northland). These are not abstract ideas to me. They are lived values. They influence how I work, how I lead, how I listen, and how I respond when life becomes demanding. They guide how I carry myself when the pressure rises and when decisions hold weight.

The teachings of my father remain present in every chapter, whether spoken directly or not. He was a Māori Warden, a man who served his community with humility, steadiness, and mana (prestige and authority). His quiet leadership taught me that real strength does not need to announce itself. His example showed me that respect is earned through action, consistency, and care for others. The courage of my mother lives just as strongly within me. She carved space for herself in a place that did not welcome her easily, choosing patience and integrity over resistance. Her strength surfaces in me whenever life tests my resolve.

This book is also fuelled by the love I hold for my children and grandchildren. They became my greatest teachers. They reminded me of what truly matters when ambition, pressure, and expectation threaten to pull focus away from what is essential. They showed me that legacy is not measured by what you build or accumulate, but by who you raise, how you show up, and the values you pass forward. And even though oceans now lie between me and my siblings, our connection remains intact. Distance does not weaken whakapapa (genealogy). Blood, memory, and shared love endure. The spirit of our parents keeps us connected, no matter how far apart we stand.

I wrote this book for anyone who has ever felt different. For anyone who struggled with a speech stammer or felt their voice trapped inside. For anyone who lost confidence along the way. For anyone who made mistakes they wish they could rewrite. For anyone who had to rebuild themselves later in life, quietly and without permission. For anyone who felt too old, too tired, or too far behind to begin again. For anyone who carries dreams but has not yet allowed themselves to believe those dreams are still possible.

If any part of that feels familiar, this book is written with you in mind.

You will not find a superhero in these pages. You will find a man who kept going. A man who stumbled, failed, learned, forgave, rebuilt, and refused to stop swimming, even when the water was cold, dark, and unfamiliar. What I have learned through every chapter is this. Your voice can be found. Your future can be reshaped. Your spirit can be renewed at any age. Your potential does not expire with time. Curiosity can return. Purpose can reignite. Direction can emerge even after long periods of doubt.

This is my story, but it is offered as a companion to yours.

To walk beside you.
To steady you when the ground shifts.
To remind you that even an imperfect journey can become a meaningful one.

So turn the page. Step into the chapters ahead with an open heart.
Take what you need.
Leave what you do not.
And remember, no matter where you are starting from.

Keep swimming.

Your next chapter is already waiting.

CHAPTER 1

Part 1: A Childhood Held Together by Whānau and Courage

I grew up in Inglewood, a small New Zealand town shaped by simplicity and community, the kind of place where life unfolded at an unhurried pace and people still trusted one another enough to leave doors unlocked. It was the sort of town where neighbours did not feel like strangers but like extended family, where you could wander into someone's kitchen without knocking and be handed a biscuit before anyone asked why you were there. The rhythm of life was steady and predictable, guided more by seasons and shared routines than by schedules, ambition, or urgency. Nothing felt rushed. Nothing felt disposable. Life simply happened, and everyone seemed to be moving at roughly the same speed.

Inglewood had a sound of its own. On some mornings it was birds arguing in the trees like they were holding a committee meeting without a chairperson. On others it was the thud of a rugby ball being kicked around on damp grass, the squeak of a screen door opening and closing, or someone calling across a fence as if distance was optional. It smelled like freshly cut hay in summer, wet wool in winter, and the faint promise of rain that Inglewood never really lets go of. Even now, decades later, if I catch the smell of grass after rain, it takes me straight back. Not to a specific moment, but to a feeling. The feeling of being held by a place that knew you.

The town ran on unspoken agreements that cities seem to forget. If someone's car would not start, a neighbour appeared with jumper leads and a confident opinion about what you were doing wrong. If a kid scraped a knee, an aunty rinsed it, patched it, and sent him back outside with a warning that sounded stern but was actually care. Adults watched everyone's children as if it was their responsibility, and in many ways it was. You did not need security cameras when you had neighbours who could see trouble forming from behind half closed curtains. If you thought you were getting away with something, you were usually mistaken, and you would find out later that evening when your mother already knew what you had done.

I was the second eldest of four children in a Māori (Indigenous people of New Zealand) family, born into a life filled with laughter, noise, cultural grounding, and an abundance of love that never needed explanation. Our household was not quiet. It was alive. Conversations overlapped. Music drifted through rooms. People came and went without ceremony. And somehow, through all of that movement, there was a deep sense of safety. You knew you belonged. You felt it without needing to be told.

We lived with a kind of practical warmth. It was never fancy, but it was real. Clothes were handed down, repaired, and handed down again, which is a polite way of saying most of us were wearing history. Food was stretched. Money was managed carefully. Yet somehow, there was always enough. Not enough for luxury, but enough for laughter. Enough for a full belly. Enough for one more kid at the table when someone arrived hungry and nobody bothered asking why.

My siblings and I were raised inside a close knit circle of family and whānau (extended family). Cousins were not occasional visitors. They were constants, as familiar as siblings and just as involved in our everyday lives. We grew up together, played together, fought together, and learned together. Boundaries were tested daily, usually followed by laughter, sometimes followed by a telling off from whichever adult happened to be closest at the time.

Sometimes the telling off came from the person you least expected. You might think you were safe because Mum was not around, then suddenly an aunty would appear with that look that could stop you mid sentence. The look said she knew exactly what you were doing and was not impressed. She would follow it with a sentence that sounded casual but carried authority. Put that back. Go and sort it out. Take your shoes off in my house. Even then, you never doubted you were loved. Discipline was not about embarrassment. It was about alignment. It was about reminding you who you were and who you represented.

Within the Māori (Indigenous people of New Zealand) community, identity was not something you questioned. It was lived. My Māori mates were my brothers. They were the ones I ran with, scraped knees with, shared secrets with, and got into trouble with, then blamed each other for, and then somehow all ended up forgiven anyway. Alongside them were my Pākehā (European New Zealanders) mates, who blended seamlessly into our lives. Culture was not divided. It was shared. Differences existed, but they were not barriers. They were simply part of the environment, like weather or landscape.

From an early age, I understood that my bloodline ran in more than one direction, like rivers meeting before flowing into the same sea. My father was Ngāti Porou (tribe from the East Coast of New Zealand), raised within a large East Coast whānau (extended family) where whakapapa (genealogy) was spoken with familiarity and pride. Even though I did not grow up surrounded by every member of that side of the family, the stories travelled to me naturally. They arrived in fragments, in anecdotes, in quiet references that carried more meaning than explanation ever could.

Whakapapa (genealogy) in our world was not just information. It was orientation. It told you where you came from, who stood behind you, and what you carried forward. It was not about status. It was about connection. It was the difference between feeling like a single person in the world and knowing you belonged to a long line of people who had survived challenges you had not yet faced.

I met my grandfather briefly. The encounter was short, but it left an impression that lingered. There was weight in his presence, a sense of authority that did not need to be asserted. In the years that followed, stories about him filled the gaps. His strength. His humour. His sharp wit. That particular East Coast resilience that seemed to come not just from upbringing, but from the land itself. It felt as though the cliffs and coastline had shaped the men who came from them, carving steadiness and resolve into their character.

My great grandfather on that side came from England, a reminder that whakapapa is rarely simple. It is layered, complex, and often incomplete until you take the time to explore it. I never met him. I knew him only through a photograph, his face frozen in time, offering no voice, no story of his own. For many years, that absence felt like a closed door. Only later, when I recieved our family tree from whanau (family), did I realise that silence can also be a form of connection. Through those searches, I discovered English and French roots that expanded my understanding of where I came from.

These discoveries did not dilute my sense of self. They broadened it. Our lineage carried multiple histories within it. Māori blood and colonial blood flowed side by side. There were stories of conflict and stories of cooperation, stories of loss and stories of survival. These histories did not align neatly, but they coexisted, shaping generations quietly, often without being spoken aloud. It helped me understand identity not as a single thread, but as a weaving formed over time by movement, circumstance, and choice.

Even with that understanding, the Māori side of my identity remained the strongest pull. It was the rhythm I returned to when things felt uncertain. It shaped how I understood responsibility, community, and resilience. It taught me that strength does not need to announce itself and that connection to people and place matters more than recognition or status.

My mother was Ngā Puhi (tribe from Northland), and her story carried lessons of endurance and grace that shaped our family deeply. She lost both of her parents at a young age, leaving her to navigate the world without the guidance most children rely on. Yet their absence did not erase their influence. She spoke of them often. Their values. Their sacrifices. Their importance. Though they were not present in years, they were present in spirit.

Alongside her Ngā Puhi heritage, my mother also carried Portuguese roots, another layer of whakapapa (genealogy) that lived quietly within her. It surfaced in stories, in mannerisms, and in the unspoken strength she showed during hardship. Identity, for her, was not something to defend loudly. It was something to live consistently.

When she moved to Taranaki, she entered a place where history had a long memory. Old tensions between Ngā Puhi (tribe) and Taranaki Māori (Indigenous people of New Zealand) lingered beneath the surface. My mother arrived fully aware that she was an outsider, both geographically and culturally. She met suspicion with patience. She met distance with warmth. She did not demand acceptance. She allowed trust to grow.

Over time, the community softened. She was embraced as whānau (family). Her presence became familiar. Her contribution valued. Watching her taught me that belonging is not claimed. It is earned through consistency, humility, and integrity.

Growing up between Ngāti Porou and Ngā Puhi gave me a deep understanding of whānau. Family extended beyond parents and siblings. Aunties and uncles held authority. Elders watched over everyone. Accountability was constant. You could not disappear. If you stepped out of line, someone noticed.

My parents were the foundation of everything I became. My father carried a tireless work ethic that needed no announcement. He showed up. He did what needed to be done. His approval came rarely, but when it did, it mattered. My mother was the heart of the home. Music flowed constantly. Dad played guitar. Mum sang. I often fell asleep next to my father as he played, feeling the vibration of the strings through the wood.

Aunty Kim brought colour and magic into our lives. She softened rules and expanded imagination. One of her greatest tricks was turning a black and white television into colour using plastic film. To us, it worked perfectly.

Our childhood lived outdoors. The river was our playground. Cold, clear, alive. We drifted between houses, ate from each other's cupboards, and ran through backyards as if they belonged to all of us.

I had a stutter. With whānau, it did not matter. With strangers, it did. Sport became my escape. Music became another freedom. At eight years old, standing under bright lights in the Inglewood Town Hall singing Ben by Michael Jackson, I felt no fear.

Inglewood gave me roots. It gave me belonging. It gave me identity before I had language for it. The boy I was there would one day become the man who learned to rebuild himself again and again.

CHAPTER 1

Part 2: Learning the World Through Rivers, Music and Mischief

If there was a single place that shaped my childhood almost as much as my own home, it was the river. That long ribbon of cold, clear water winding its way through Inglewood, moving patiently through the landscape as if it had always been there and always would be. It glinted in the sun on bright days and darkened under cloud, changing character with the seasons, yet never losing its pull on us. To us kids, it felt like it had been placed there just for us. The river was our playground, our classroom, our proving ground. It was where we learned courage, competition, balance, and fearlessness without ever naming those lessons. It was where scraped knees, bruised elbows, and swallowed mouthfuls of water quietly toughened us up. We tested ourselves daily without ever calling it a test.

We learned quickly which stones were slick with moss and would send you flying if you stepped carelessly. We learned which currents were stronger than they looked and could drag you sideways when you least expected it. We learned which calm-looking stretches dropped away suddenly into deep, dark water that demanded respect. The river taught awareness. It taught humility. You didn't just play in it; you learned to read it. And if you failed to read it properly, you paid for it with fear, embarrassment, or a hard lesson that stayed with you.

That river raised us almost as much as our parents did. It shaped our bodies, hardened our legs, strengthened our lungs, and sharpened our instincts. It taught us confidence without arrogance and respect without fear. You didn't conquer the river. You learned how to move with it, how to listen to it, how to trust it without ever taking it for granted.

We would leave the house in the morning barefoot, half dressed, hair still wild from sleep, already laughing before the day had properly begun. Breakfast was optional. Shoes were unnecessary. The sound of our voices echoed down the street as we ran. We never knew who would join us on any given day. Cousins. Neighbours. Māori (Indigenous people of New Zealand) kids. Pākehā (white / non-Māori New Zealanders) kids. Kids from up the road who heard the noise and followed it like a call. The group shifted constantly, growing and shrinking as people came and went. There was no plan, no clock, no adult supervision hovering nearby. Just the river, the sun, and our imaginations stretching out ahead of us.

By midday, the group had usually doubled in size, as if the river itself was drawing children in. Parents trusted the river because it had already raised generations before us. Everyone knew where we were, even if no one could say exactly what we were doing.

Dad taught me how to swim there. Not in a heated pool with lane ropes, tiled floors, and a coach's whistle cutting through the air, but in water that demanded attention and respect. Nature was the instructor, and Dad was the guide. He would launch himself into the river like it was a warm bath, even when it was so cold it shocked the breath from your chest. He splashed, laughed, dived beneath us, surfaced unexpectedly, grabbed us, spun us, and tossed us across the water as if we were weightless. Fear dissolved around him. He made the river feel safe even when it wasn't. That was his gift.

Dad had a quiet power about him, a steady presence that didn't need to announce itself. He didn't say much, but when he did, you listened. His calm wrapped around you like a shield. If he was nearby, you believed everything would be all right, even when logic suggested otherwise.

And when we weren't at the river, we were often at the sea.

The ocean was a different teacher altogether. Bigger. Louder. Less forgiving. Older than anything we could comprehend. The sea didn't care who you were. It demanded respect immediately. Its moods shifted quickly, from calm and inviting to wild and dangerous in moments. The sea carried its own rules, its own rhythms, and its own stories passed down through generations.

As a whānau (extended family), we went together. Not just to play, but to gather kai (food). These trips were about more than enjoyment. They were about survival, tradition, and connection. Sea urchins, pāua (abalone), and mussels clung stubbornly to the rocks, and we learned how to find them, how to pry them free carefully, and how not to damage the reef in the process. We learned patience. We learned restraint. We learned that taking too much was never acceptable.

We would eat our fill right there, standing on rocks slick with seawater, salt on our lips, hands numb from the cold, the smell of the ocean clinging to our skin. Then we would gather the rest and take it home to share. Food from the sea was never just food. It was connection to the land and water. It was responsibility. It was whakapapa (genealogy / lineage) made tangible through action. Knowledge wasn't written down; it was lived.

Those trips were never rushed. Elders watched closely, correcting gently, teaching through example rather than instruction. You were shown which areas were safe and which were not. Some places were tapu (sacred or forbidden). Certain rocks, pools, or stretches of water carried stories of taniwha (mythical guardian or water spirit). These weren't treated as fairy tales. Whether you fully understood them or not, you listened. You respected the warnings. You didn't mock them. You didn't test them.

Māori culture teaches that the land and sea are alive, that they remember, and that they respond to how they are treated. Even as children, we felt that truth. There was an unspoken understanding that some boundaries were not ours to cross. Respect wasn't optional; it was expected.

Back at the riverbank, we played cowboy and Indians, and without fail I was always the Indian. Something about it felt right, even then. I liked the speed, the war cries, the grit. I liked the feeling of being wild, agile, and free. I liked the sense of connection to something older than myself, something deeper. I didn't have the language for it at the time, but there was a spiritual thread running through that choice. I was choosing identity long before I understood what identity truly meant.

When we weren't in the water, we were exploring. Chasing each other through long grass, hiding in reeds, throwing sticks, climbing trees, daring each other higher and higher. We argued about who got to be leader, then forgot the argument minutes later. The day flowed without structure, guided only by hunger, tiredness, or the fading light.

And when we tired of that, we roamed between houses as if the entire neighbourhood was one big home. Our neighbours' kids were family in everything but name. There was no sharp line between whose house was whose. Doors were open. Fridges were shared. We drifted in and out without knocking, as if every home belonged to everyone.

One minute you were in your own kitchen, the next you were sitting cross-legged on a neighbour's floor, halfway through a conversation that had started somewhere else entirely. We ate whatever was available and never questioned it. Biscuits from one house. Fruit from another. Toast thick with butter and jam wherever you landed. No one asked which child belonged to which house. It didn't matter. Everyone knew everyone. Everyone looked out for everyone.

That was childhood. Shaped by river and sea. Fed by land and ocean. Grounded in whānau (family), respect, and stories older than us.

Those waters didn't just surround our lives; they formed them, carried us forward, and left their imprint on who we would become.

The street itself felt alive. It watched over us. Parents kept an eye out without hovering. If you stepped out of line at one end of the road, word would reach your house before you did. Neighbour kids were not just playmates. They were cousins in practice, if not by blood. If someone scraped a knee, any adult nearby would step in. If you were hungry, someone would feed you. If you stayed out too long, someone would send you home. Responsibility was shared, and so was care.

Almost every household had a dog, and those dogs were as much a part of the community as the people. They roamed free all day, every day, moving from house to house as if on their own schedule. No fences. No leads. Just familiarity. It was not unusual to be walking home from school and, at the top of the street, see a pack of dogs waiting. Ten of them sometimes, tails wagging, running together up the road to meet you like a welcoming committee. They knew the sound of school bags. They knew the rhythm of the day. You would be greeted before you even reached your own gate.

Those dogs followed us everywhere. They lay in the shade while we played. They trailed behind us on bikes and foot races. They slept on doorsteps and under tables. They belonged everywhere and nowhere all at once. Their presence added to the feeling that the street was safe, watched over, and full of life. Even when adults were busy, it never felt empty.

That sense of belonging is rare. You do not realise it while you are living inside it. It feels normal. It feels ordinary. It is only when you grow older and look back that you understand how special it was. How few people ever experience a community where doors are open, food is shared without question, children are raised collectively, and even the dogs know where they belong.

What we had was more than a neighbourhood. It was a shared life. And once you have known that kind of community, it stays with you. You carry it quietly, measuring every place you live afterward against the feeling of being known, welcomed, and watched over without needing to ask.

And then there were the eeling nights. They were never rushed and never accidental. This was not something you did on a whim after dinner. It was usually a weekend venture, planned with care and precision. There was an unspoken understanding of who was going, what gear was needed, and when the timing was right. The river dictated the rules. You learned to listen to it, to respect it, and to move with it rather than against it.

We would head down as the light softened, carrying lines, spears, or gaffs, already slipping into a quieter mindset. One of the first lessons you learned was to walk your way upstream. You always positioned yourself so the disturbed water stayed behind you. Dirty water downstream meant clearer water ahead, and clearer water meant better chances. It was practical knowledge passed down through doing, not instruction. You learned quickly or you went home empty handed.

We would feel along the banks with our hands, slow and careful, reaching into dark hollows where the eels liked to hide. Sometimes your fingers brushed mud or roots. Sometimes they brushed something that moved. When you felt that thick, slick body shift beneath your hand, your heart jumped. Some of those eels were enormous, a metre long, sometimes a metre and a half. Powerful. Ancient. You felt their strength even before you saw them.

There was hierarchy in everything we did. Someone handled the spear or the gaff. That role was earned, not given. Experience mattered. Precision mattered. One wrong move and the eel was gone. The youngest usually had a different job. Carrying the eels once they were landed. It was heavy work, awkward and messy, but it was part of learning your place. Everyone contributed. Everyone mattered.

The anticipation was its own adventure. Standing still. Watching the water. Feeling the cold creep in as the night settled. Then the moment came. A tug on the line. A sudden movement in the water. Everything snapped into focus. Hands moved fast. Voices dropped. The eel came up fighting, twisting, surprising you every time with its weight and power. You never forgot how strong they were.

We took them home to clean, and that was its own ritual. Cutting. Gutting. Preparing them for cooking. It was messy, slippery, smelly work, and no one pretended otherwise. Yet it felt important. Like tradition being passed from one set of hands to another. This was more than food gathering. It was connection. To the river. To each other. To something older than all of us.

We always shared the catch with local Māori families. Not because anyone told us to. Not because it was expected. But because that was simply the way things were done. You did not keep abundance to yourself. You passed it on. Sharing was not charity. It was culture. It was respect. It was an understanding that what you took from the land and water was never just yours to keep.

Those nights stayed with me. The planning. The patience. The hierarchy. The shared work. The shared reward. They taught me lessons about preparation, responsibility, and generosity long before I had words for them. Lessons that reached far beyond the riverbank and followed me quietly into the rest of my life.

Those days built me. Those days shaped the framework of how I would later navigate the world. There is something about growing up in a small town with deep roots that stays inside you no matter where you go. It teaches you to trust people. To value relationships. To see the good in simplicity. To show up for others without being asked.

And in the midst of all that freedom and noise and childhood adventure, my voice struggled to keep up.

My stammer was something I did not fully understand at the time, and for a long while, I did not even have the language to describe it. I do not know exactly when it began or how old I was when it first appeared. There was no clear starting point, no single moment where it suddenly arrived. It simply existed. As far back as I can remember, it was already there, present even in my earliest memories of pre-school. Long before I understood fear, performance, or self-consciousness, my voice carried its own struggle.

At that age, I did not think of it as a stammer. I just knew that sometimes the words would not come out the way I wanted them to. Sounds would catch in my mouth. Syllables would repeat or stop altogether. I would know exactly what I wanted to say, but my body refused to cooperate. It was confusing and frustrating, especially because I did not yet understand why it was happening or how to stop it.

It was not constant, and that made it even harder to make sense of. Some days my speech flowed easily, and other days it felt like every sentence was an obstacle. It was unpredictable. It flared around strangers, teachers, and anyone outside my comfortable circle. But it did not stop there. Even with family, with my parents, with people who loved me, I struggled. I wanted to speak freely to them. I wanted to answer questions, tell stories, explain myself. Instead, I would feel the words jam in my throat, stuck halfway between thought and sound.

Sentences stumbled. Sounds locked themselves in place. The more I tried to push them out, the worse it became. I could feel the frustration build in my chest, tight and heavy. My cheeks would flush as embarrassment crept in. I could see people waiting for me to finish, their patience kind but noticeable, and that awareness only made it harder. As a child, you want to be heard quickly. You want to keep up. You want to be part of the moment. My voice often slowed me down.

What made the difference was how the people around me responded. Around cousins, mates, family, and neighbours, it did not matter. They let me finish. They did not rush me. They did not complete my sentences for me. They did not tease me or make me feel smaller for struggling. They treated my voice as if it were completely normal, as if the pauses and repetitions were simply part of who I was.

That acceptance mattered more than I could have known at the time. It gave me space. It allowed me to breathe. It taught me, quietly, that my worth was not measured by how smoothly I spoke. Even when I felt frustrated with myself, the people around me never made my voice feel like a problem that needed fixing. They listened. And because they listened, I learned that even a difficult voice still deserved to be heard.

Those early experiences stayed with me. They shaped how I understood patience, empathy, and belonging. They showed me that being allowed to finish a sentence can be an act of kindness, and that sometimes the most powerful support is simply giving someone the time they need to find their words.

Running gave me relief. Sprinting across the school field or tearing along the riverbank gave me the feeling of control that speaking sometimes took away. When I ran, I didn't think. I didn't hesitate. I didn't fight myself. I just moved. And movement became its own language.

That night planted something inside me. A sense of possibility. A sense that even if I struggled in one area, I could excel in another. And maybe that is the balance life gives us without explaining it.

My brother was another kind of inspiration. He excelled in sport and academics. He did everything with ease. When he walked onto a stage to collect trophies, he looked like he belonged there. He was someone people admired. I admired him more than anyone. And even though I never said it out loud, he set the benchmark for the kind of person I wanted to become.

There is something powerful about growing up in the shadow of excellence. It could crush you or sharpen you. For me, it sharpened me.

Life in Inglewood gave me something many people spend their whole lives searching for. A beginning built on stability, culture, identity, belonging and love. A childhood full of laughter and scraped knees and muddy feet and songs floating through the evening air.

Those first years shaped every chapter that came after. The lessons were simple, but the impact was huge. From rivers to eeling nights, from singing on stage to running cross country, from stuttering in class to yelling war cries with my mates, everything was part of the foundation.

Inglewood didn't just raise me.
It prepared me.

For challenges I didn't know were coming.
For reinventions I didn't yet understand.
For a life that would take me far beyond that small town, and yet always lead me back to the boy who learned courage there.

CHAPTER 1

Part 3: The Shy Kid Who Ran Faster Than His
Voice

By the time I reached the middle years of primary school, I had already learned that I carried two very different versions of myself inside the same body. They lived side by side, switching places depending on where I was and who was watching. One version felt effortless, almost natural. The other required courage just to exist.

There was the bold version of me. The one who roared with my cousins as we sprinted through open fields, grass whipping against our legs, lungs burning with laughter. The one who hurled himself into the river without hesitation, staying in the water until our bodies shook uncontrollably from the cold. The one who climbed hay bales stacked high in paddocks, leapt from tree branches like we were immune to gravity, and lived with the full belief that nothing could stop us. That boy was loud, fearless, wild, and unstoppable. That boy could outrun almost anyone, outshout anyone during a game, and take on any challenge put in front of him without a second thought.

Movement was where that version of me lived. In motion, I was confident. In motion, I was powerful. In motion, I belonged.

Then there was the other version.

The quieter one. The one who froze when a teacher called my name unexpectedly. The one whose heart thumped hard against his ribs when asked to read aloud or answer a question. The one who felt his throat tighten the moment he tried to speak to someone new. The one whose stutter wrapped itself around his words like vines around a fence, stopping sentences before they could fully grow. That boy felt smaller. More fragile. More exposed. He was still me, just stripped of movement, left standing still with nothing to hide behind.

That version only appeared when I had to speak.

The contrast between those two versions of myself created a strange tension inside me. At home, or with my whānau (extended family), I was confident, loud, and expressive. My words flowed freely because I felt safe. But at school, surrounded by classmates I didn't know deeply or teachers who didn't quite understand what a stutter really felt like from the inside, I became acutely aware of my voice. Every sentence felt like a risk. Every answer felt like a test I might fail.

Kids can be cruel without meaning to be. Some laughed outright. Some mimicked sounds they didn't understand. Some stared at the floor while I struggled to finish a sentence. Others waited impatiently, tapping fingers, shifting weight, eager for me to hurry up. Even when they tried to be kind, I could feel the tension in the room. That quiet pressure made me swallow words instead of speaking them. Silence became easier than effort.

But running changed everything.

Running was my escape. My freedom. My power. When I ran, I wasn't the boy who stuttered. I wasn't the kid who hesitated or froze. I wasn't the one tripping over syllables and sounds. I was the leader. The one out in front. The one setting the pace. The one whose legs moved faster than doubt could ever catch up with me.

I didn't run because someone told me to. I ran because something inside me needed it. Something in my legs, something in my lungs, something in my heart demanded release. Running felt like truth. And the more I ran, the more the teachers noticed. Suddenly I was being entered into races. Cross-country events. Sprints. Relays. Inter-school competitions. I didn't just participate. I started winning.

I started hearing my name called out in assemblies for reasons that had nothing to do with speaking. Applause replaced awkward silence. Pride replaced fear. It was the first time I felt publicly strong, publicly valued, publicly seen.

And that mattered.

Because the world doesn't offer shy kids many public victories. But sport gave me mine.

Even outside of organised sport, movement defined my days. We ran everywhere, barefoot most of the time, our feet toughened by gravel roads, tree roots, paddock dirt, and river stones. Shoes were for school or church, not for living. We chased each other until our lungs burned and our legs wobbled. We raced up and down paddocks behind our houses. We sprinted to the dairy and back just to prove who was fastest that afternoon.

That kind of upbringing built something deep inside me. Resilience. A tough skin. A refusal to crumble under pressure. When life later threw challenges I couldn't outrun, my childhood had already trained me to keep moving forward anyway.

But my early years weren't shaped by sport and stuttering alone.

There was music, too.

Music was the thread that wove our home together. My father strumming the guitar. My mother singing harmonies effortlessly. My cousins clapping rhythms, singing whatever came to mind, turning ordinary evenings into moments of magic. We didn't need an audience or an occasion. Music wasn't something we performed. It was something we lived.

That love for music gave me courage in a way nothing else could. Singing bypassed the broken bridges in my speech. It allowed me to express emotion without fear. When I sang, the stutter lost its grip.

Melody smoothed what words struggled to deliver. Music became another safe place, another form of freedom.

Primary school was full of moments like that. Small victories. Hidden battles. Quiet fears. Unexpected triumphs. My teachers didn't always understand the stutter, but many of them saw beyond it. They pushed me where I was strong. They encouraged my running. They applauded my singing. They recognised confidence even when my voice stumbled.

But the biggest lessons never happened inside classrooms.

They happened in the moments between. Playing on asphalt courts with my Māori (Indigenous people of New Zealand) mates. Sitting on the grass with my Pākehā (white / non-Māori New Zealanders) friends. Trading sandwiches and secrets. Laughing over nothing. Learning loyalty. Learning trust. Learning how to belong.

Those early friendships were real bonds, formed before the world taught us to put up walls. We shared everything. Food. Shoes. Toys. Tears. Victories. Losses. No one was left out. No one walked alone.

Family added even more layers to who I was becoming. My older brother remained the lighthouse I chased, always just ahead of me, giving me something to aim for and sometimes to beat. My sister and I fought and laughed in equal measure, rivals and allies depending on the day. My younger brother was the baby we couldn't avoid even when we tried, clinging to Mum, clinging to us, clinging to life with the unshakeable certainty of a child who knows he is deeply loved.

Each of these people shaped me in ways I didn't understand at the time.

And through it all, my stutter was present but never defining. It was part of my story, not the whole story. Maybe that's why I never saw myself as broken. No one around me treated me as fragile. I was simply Jay. Loud when I wanted to be. Quiet when I needed to be. Fast on my feet. Sometimes slow with my words. Always surrounded by love.

Looking back now, I can see how those early years carved the foundation of my entire life. Courage wrapped in humility. Resilience wrapped in humour. Strength wrapped in vulnerability. A childhood built not on material things, but on presence, laughter, community, and whānau (family).

I didn't know it then, but I was already learning the tools I would rely on through every future chapter. Tools I would use through storms, reinventions, failures, and triumphs.

And the boy running barefoot through paddocks and riversides was slowly growing into the young man who would soon face the next stage of life.

A stage where everything would become bigger, harder, louder, and far more defining.

CHAPTER 1

Part 4: Where Confidence Begins and Identity
Takes Shape

Growing up in Inglewood felt like standing at the meeting point of
two different worlds, never fully inside one or the other, yet
permanently shaped by both. It was like having one foot planted
firmly on familiar ground while the other hovered over something
wider, more uncertain, and harder to read. I did not have language for
it at the time, but even as a child I could feel the difference. I could
feel when I was safe, and I could feel when I was exposed.

One world was warm, noisy, and alive with constant motion. It was
the world of family and whānau (extended family). Of cousins who
felt more like brothers and sisters than relatives. Of mates who turned
up every day without needing an invitation, as if presence itself was
permission enough. It was a world filled with laughter that spilled
out of houses and onto the street, voices overlapping, radios playing,
doors opening and closing without ceremony. In that world, identity
was assumed, not questioned. You belonged before you ever had to
explain who you were or where you came from. Your place was
already held for you.

The other world was broader, quieter, and far more intimidating. It
was made up of classrooms and corridors, teachers and rules,
strangers and expectations that were rarely spoken aloud but were
always present in the air. It was structured and measured, full of
invisible lines you were expected to stay within. This world asked
things of you. It assessed you. Watched you. Weighed you. It did not
know your story, and it did not slow down to learn it.

That duality settled into me early, long before I had the words to
describe it. It shaped how I spoke, how I moved, and how I learned
to navigate people and places. I became aware, instinctively, that

different versions of myself were required depending on where I stood.

Within my own environment, I felt strong. Protected. Known. Surrounded by people who had watched me grow from the beginning, who understood my silences just as much as my laughter, I carried a deep sense of belonging. It wrapped itself around me like armour. In that space, I felt free to explore, to test limits, to push boundaries, and to make mistakes without fear of being judged or cast out. I could fall, get up, and keep going.

In that world, my stammer did not define me. Pauses were accepted. Time was given. No one rushed me or finished my sentences for me. My voice was allowed to arrive in its own time. My world was patient with me, and that patience gave me room to breathe, to exist, to grow without apology. I was not broken there. I was simply me.

But the moment I stepped beyond that familiar circle, the armour grew thinner.

School felt like another country altogether. The rules were different. The rhythm was different. The expectations were sharper and less forgiving. Desks felt confining, locking bodies into stillness when every instinct in me wanted movement. The blackboard felt less like a place of learning and more like a place of exposure. Standing out front, being asked to speak, felt like being placed under a spotlight without warning.

Teachers were not unkind, but they represented authority and expectation, and expectation amplified everything I was uncertain about. When my name was called, my body reacted before my mind could catch up. My chest tightened. My breathing changed. My thoughts raced ahead of my voice, tripping over each other as they tried to get out. Sometimes the words followed. Sometimes they did not.

When they didn't, the silence felt enormous. Heavy. Stretched. Public. I could feel eyes on me, waiting. That waiting pressed down on my chest, made the words even harder to find. Each second felt like a minute. Each pause felt like failure. I hated how those moments shrank me, how they reduced me to something smaller than I knew I was inside.

Yet even then, something in me refused to retreat.

Even as my voice faltered, my body found another way to speak. Movement became my refuge. Running, sprinting, cross country, climbing, swimming, and sport in all its forms gave me a sense of alignment that words could not. When I moved, everything made sense. There was no hesitation. No translation required. My body knew what to do long before doubt could intervene.

On the field or at the river, I felt whole. Movement allowed me to express confidence without explanation, strength without words. People responded to that instinctively. They saw capability before they heard my voice. In those moments, I was not the boy who struggled to speak. I was the boy who led the race. The one out in front. The one others chased.

That contrast became one of my earliest lessons in identity. I learned that weakness and strength often sit side by side inside the same person. That you do not wait until every part of yourself feels secure before stepping forward. You move with what you have, and you trust that the rest will catch up later.

Moments began to appear where that physical confidence shifted how others saw me. Racing older boys and outrunning their expectations showed me that assumptions could be overturned. That quiet determination could outperform noise and bravado. That effort mattered more than reputation. Speed became more than a physical attribute. It became release. A way to burn off frustration, embarrassment, and the feeling of being held back by my own voice.

Confidence did not arrive suddenly. It was not a lightning strike or a single breakthrough moment. It built slowly, brick by brick. Through movement. Through recognition. Through small victories that stacked quietly on top of each other until one day I realised I was no longer invisible. That there was something inside me that others noticed. Something worth acknowledging. Somewhere along the way, I began to sense that there was more within me waiting to be unlocked.

Music played its own role in that awakening.

Singing at a young age left a mark I did not fully understand at the time. It showed me that even with a stutter, I could still shine. Music did not demand precision in the way speech did. It did not punish hesitation. It asked for feeling, rhythm, and presence. When I sang, my voice found a different pathway out of me. One that did not get tangled. One that felt free.

As I grew older, music stayed with me. It followed me through school corridors, around the dinner table, into family gatherings and quiet moments at home. Where my spoken voice sometimes betrayed me, music never did. It gave me a way to be heard without fear. A way to express emotion without explanation.

At the same time, I watched those around me closely.

My brother stood tall in my eyes, not because he demanded attention, but because he embodied something I wanted to grow into. Confidence. Capability. Direction. I absorbed everything. How he moved. How he carried himself. How he earned respect without forcing it. He gave me a target, something to chase, not through pressure but through example.

I was always looking ahead. Wondering what the next boundary was. What the next challenge might be. How far I could go if I kept pushing. That forward pull lived inside me constantly, a quiet restlessness that refused to let me settle for comfort alone.

Home life grounded all of this. It was loud, loving, chaotic, and perfectly imperfect. Mum brought discipline wrapped in warmth. Dad carried humour and gentle authority that never needed to be enforced. Aunty Kim injected imagination, energy, and freedom into ordinary days, turning the mundane into something memorable. Each of them shaped me in ways I would only fully understand decades later. Together, they created a foundation strong enough to explore from, without ever losing my footing.

If I close my eyes now, I can still feel it. That sense of being held while also being challenged. That balance between safety and curiosity. That constant pull toward what came next.

Because the truth is, the boy who ran faster than his voice, who struggled to speak around strangers but moved freely in open spaces, who navigated Māori (Indigenous people of New Zealand) and Pākehā (white / non-Māori New Zealanders) worlds without fully understanding either, who tested boundaries simply to see how far they could stretch, who learned courage at the river and resilience in classrooms, was already preparing to become something more.

He just did not know it yet.

Every moment mattered. Fear sharpened awareness. Embarrassment built humility. Victory planted belief. Belonging taught responsibility. Each experience added strength to the mind and heart. Each one stitched resilience into my character. None of it was wasted.

The boy growing up in Inglewood carried more than memories forward. He carried heart. He carried culture. He carried whānau (family). He carried curiosity. He carried grit. He carried the courage to keep moving even when unsure, even when uncomfortable, even when his voice trembled.

And beneath all of it, he carried a spark. A quiet knowing that this was only the beginning.

The shaping.
The forging.
The grounding.

Before high school.
Before London.
Before Glluz.
Before GlluzTech.
Before reinvention after reinvention.

This was where the story truly began.

CHAPTER 2

Part 1: The Shock of High School and the Birth of Reinvention

The first day of high school hits every kid differently, and you can see it written all over their faces if you know what to look for. Some walk through the gates tall, shoulders back, already sure of themselves, as if they have rehearsed the moment their entire lives. They move with confidence, laughing too loudly, claiming space before anyone can challenge them. Others shrink instinctively, eyes down, hoping not to be noticed, blending into walls, lockers, and crowds as if invisibility might offer protection. Some pretend they do not care at all, masking nerves with bravado, even though their stomach is doing somersaults and their palms are slick with sweat.

I walked in feeling like I had been transported to another planet. It was as if I had been dropped into a place that looked familiar on the surface but felt completely foreign underneath. The buildings resembled schools I had known, the routines looked recognisable, yet nothing truly fit. The scale was wrong. The energy was wrong. Even the air felt different, heavier somehow, charged with expectation and uncertainty.

Primary school had been familiar, safe, predictable in ways you only appreciate once they are gone. It had a rhythm you understood without effort. You knew every teacher by name, voice, and temperament. You knew which ones demanded discipline, which ones used humour, which ones you could quietly test, and which ones you never dared cross. You knew where every classroom was, how long it took to get there, and which shortcuts mattered when the bell rang. You knew which kids were fast, which were funny, which were trouble, and which ones would stand beside you when things got messy. You understood the unspoken rules of belonging. You felt rooted in it, held by it, protected by familiarity.

High school dismantled that sense of certainty almost immediately.

The buildings were bigger and colder, designed for movement and control rather than comfort. Corridors echoed when you walked through them, amplifying every footstep and making you feel smaller with each step. The students were older, broader, louder, carrying themselves with an ease that came from experience. Some already looked like adults, with facial hair, deeper voices, and confidence worn like armour. Strangers were everywhere, moving past you without recognition. New rules existed, but no one explained them. Expectations hovered constantly, and you were somehow supposed to already understand how things worked. Routines shifted daily. Teachers rotated through your life, each with different standards, different energy, different tolerance.

None of them knew my face.
None of them knew my strengths.
None of them knew my stutter.

It felt like starting life from scratch again, stripped of context and history, expected to perform without introduction.

I remember walking across the courtyard that first morning with a tight knot lodged deep in my stomach. My mates were there, familiar faces from primary school, but even they seemed smaller against the scale of this new place. We clustered together instinctively, shoulders brushing, glancing around as if closeness alone might offer protection. Older students moved through the school with an ease that made it clear this was their territory. They laughed loudly, shoved casually, tested limits without fear of consequence. In many ways, they owned the place.

We were just first years, easy to spot and easier to test. Fresh faces, fresh targets, still learning where the invisible lines were drawn.

For me, the boy who had spent a childhood running free, swimming in rivers, climbing banks and trees, winning races and leading games, something shifted almost immediately. I felt hesitant in a way I had not felt in years. My steps slowed without me noticing. My shoulders tightened. The confidence I carried in open spaces did not follow me into these corridors. It stayed behind somewhere near the river, somewhere closer to home, where movement had always meant freedom.

My stutter returned more sharply in those early days, as if it too felt the pressure of unfamiliar ground.

Teachers calling the roll made my body tense before my name even reached their lips. I could feel it coming, like a wave gathering strength before it breaks. Introducing myself to new classmates made me stumble over words I had said effortlessly a hundred times before. Speaking in front of people who did not know me, who did not yet know how to wait or give space, made me retreat inward. The pauses felt longer. The silence heavier.

The confidence I carried around family, friends, and familiar ground did not travel with me into these hallways. It hovered just out of reach, something I could almost touch but never quite hold onto when I needed it most.

But that was only part of the story unfolding inside me.

Another part began to surface, a rebellious edge I had not consciously chosen but could not ignore. It arrived quietly at first, then grew bolder as the days passed. Maybe it came from pressure. Maybe from insecurity. Maybe from a need to be seen when I felt invisible. Whatever the cause, the moment someone laughed at my stutter or underestimated me, something inside me pushed back.

I started cracking jokes in class, using humour as both shield and weapon. I talked when I was not supposed to, interrupting before I could be interrupted. I sought attention instead of avoiding it, choosing visibility over silence. I pushed boundaries to see where they would bend. I tested teachers, tested rules, tested the system, and tested myself, trying to work out where I stood in this new hierarchy.

It felt like I was carving out space in a world that suddenly felt too big and unfamiliar. If I could control the narrative, even through disruption, then maybe I could control how I was seen. If they laughed with me, perhaps they would not laugh at me. If I set the tone, maybe I would not be defined by hesitation.

I was not a bad kid. I was a kid trying to find his footing on ground that felt unstable and unforgiving, using the tools he had at the time.

Then one morning shifted everything.

The day before, I had been disruptive in class. Nothing extreme or malicious, just enough to cross a line. Enough to be noticed. Enough to be sent out. The next day, I was called to the principal's office. I walked there already resigned to the outcome, rehearsing the familiar script in my head. Behave better. Focus more. Stop talking. Do better. I prepared myself to mentally switch off before he even spoke.

But that was not what happened.

He sat me down and looked at me with calm interest rather than frustration or disappointment. He spoke to me as if I mattered, as if I was someone worth investing in rather than someone who needed fixing. He told me he knew who I was. He knew my family. He had seen me on the field, watched me run, watched me play rugby. He had heard about my potential long before this moment.

Then he said something I will never forget.

"There are boys in this school who look up to you, especially our Māori (Indigenous people of New Zealand) boys. You don't realise it, but they watch everything you do. You have a choice. You can lead them somewhere good, or you can lead them somewhere bad."

He said it gently, without accusation, but the words carried weight. They landed heavily and stayed there.

He spoke about responsibility, identity, reputation, and the example I was setting whether I liked it or not. He told me I did not need to be the loudest person in the room to be respected. He told me my talent was obvious to everyone except me.

Before I left, he added something that followed me long after I walked out of his office.

"You are capable of more than you think. Stop giving us the version of yourself that hides behind jokes."

That conversation reset something inside me. It did not change me overnight, but it planted a seed. A seed that told me I could be more. A seed that suggested people saw potential even when I could not yet see it myself.

The transition into high school was still far from smooth.

Every day brought new tests. New subjects. New teachers with styles that either clicked or clashed. Classes where I felt completely out of place. Lessons that bored me. Lessons that overwhelmed me. Lessons that made me want to walk out and never look back. It was a constant process of adjusting and readjusting, learning where I fit, where I struggled, and where I needed to push harder.

Gradually, something began to shift.

The older boys who once intimidated me became benchmarks rather than threats. They were no longer obstacles to avoid but standards to measure myself against. I wanted to stand alongside them, not behind them. I wanted to earn my place through effort, discipline, and courage rather than noise or disruption.

High school stopped being only about books and classrooms. It became about identity. About discovering who I was in a much bigger, more demanding world.

Sport became my anchor in the chaos.

Rugby. Running. Athletics.

They grounded me in ways nothing else could. They gave me purpose when everything else felt uncertain. They reminded me who I was when doubt crept in. On the field and the track, my stutter did not matter. My confidence did not crack. My voice did not shake. My body spoke clearly, and effort translated directly into outcome. That made sense to me in a way little else did.

In that first year of high school, sport became more than something I did. It became how I understood myself. Every training session, every race, every game, every bruise, every victory, every loss layered together to form the early shape of the person I was becoming.

Confidence alone was not enough to survive high school. You needed grit, adaptability, heart, and resilience.

And the boy who had learned those lessons in rivers, backyards, paddocks, and bush tracks was ready for the next round.

High school was bigger.

So was I.

Even if I did not fully realise it yet.

CHAPTER 2

Part 2: The First XV, the Rise in Confidence,
and Learning That Talent Opens Doors

As the fog of my first year of high school slowly began to lift, I felt
something inside me settle in a way it hadn't before. The confusion
that had followed me through unfamiliar corridors, new classrooms,
and shifting expectations started to loosen its grip. The constant
sense of being slightly out of place no longer dominated every
moment of the day. The growing pains that came with moving
through a bigger, louder, more demanding world began to make
sense, as if my body and mind were finally catching up to the
environment around me.

Maybe it was that I had finally found my rhythm. Maybe it was the
principal's words still echoing quietly in the background, resurfacing
whenever I felt myself drifting off course. Maybe it was simply time
doing what time does best, smoothing sharp edges and allowing
confidence to take root. Whatever the reason, I could feel myself
stepping closer to who I was meant to be. Not all at once, not
dramatically, but steadily, with intention.

I was no longer just surviving high school.

I was learning how to belong in it.

Sport became the anchor that pulled me forward, the one constant
that brought order to everything else. When school felt
overwhelming, sport brought clarity. When doubt crept in, training
pushed it back out. It gave structure to my days and meaning to my
effort. It offered a space where expectations were clear and outcomes
were earned, not negotiated.

Rugby, in particular, was becoming far more than just a game. It was where I felt most alive, most certain, most myself. Something switched on inside me the moment I stepped onto a field. The smell of damp grass. The weight of the mud under my boots. The sweat building across my back as the game wore on. The solid thud of contact in a tackle. The jolt of breaking through space. The rhythm of the team moving together with shared intent. All of it made sense to me in a way classrooms sometimes did not. On the field, nothing felt forced. Everything felt earned.

I trained like I had something to prove, and in truth, I did.
Not to others, but to myself.

So when the coach began reading out names for the First XV that year, I listened only out of curiosity. I assumed the selection would follow the usual pattern. Older boys. More experienced players. Those already woven into the school's rugby culture. Names everyone expected to hear. I stood there without expectation, without anticipation, simply listening.

Then he said my name.

For a moment, everything around me went quiet. Not disbelief, but recognition. Something deeper settled in my chest. The kind of moment where time slows just long enough for you to understand that life has shifted direction. A turn you did not see coming, yet one you had unknowingly been preparing for all along.

At fourteen years old, I was one of the youngest players in the team.

Some teammates looked at me with surprise. Others with curiosity. No one said anything outright, but their glances carried questions. Do you belong here? Can you handle it? Are you ready for this level? I did not answer them with words. I answered them with effort, consistency, and performance.

Being selected changed the way people saw me almost overnight. Teachers paid closer attention. Students learned my name. Coaches invested time, belief, and expectation into me. Younger boys began watching me the way I once watched my brother, measuring themselves against what they thought was possible.

It was not fame.

It was something far more meaningful.

Validation.

And with that validation, my confidence grew. Not in loud declarations or dramatic shifts, but quietly, naturally, as if it had been waiting for permission to arrive. It settled into me without needing to be announced.

Running continued to be the foundation beneath everything else. I won cross country year after year. Sprinting sharpened my legs. Distance sharpened my lungs. Each race added another layer of belief, another reminder that effort, repeated consistently, produced results. Running became proof that discipline mattered, that showing up mattered, that patience paid off.

Athletics added another dimension to that belief. Discus. Triple jump. Events built on timing, power, rhythm, and precision. Disciplines that felt strangely natural to me. Placing third in the Taranaki Secondary Schools championships felt unreal. I stood alongside athletes who trained harder, boys who were bigger, stronger, and came from well known sporting families. Yet there I was, holding my own. It felt like confirmation that hard work could close the gap between expectation and achievement.

That belief pushed me toward something even bigger.

The Taranaki Sportsman Superstar competition.

It was designed for eighteen year olds. High level athletes only. Definitely not intended for a sixteen year old. But I entered anyway, adjusting my age on the form without hesitation. Not to cheat. Not to hide. But because I genuinely believed I could stand beside those older athletes and compete at their level.

The events were tough. The competition was fierce. The pressure was real. But I did not fold. I performed. Again and again, I surprised the judges and the older competitors. By the end of the day, I had won the entire competition.

The next morning, the newspaper exposed my lie.

Youngest winner at eighteen.

Except I was not eighteen.

Mum read it, shook her head, laughed, and said, "You little bugger." Beneath her laughter, I saw pride. Not in the rule bending, but in the belief behind it.

Those wins shaped me, not because of the trophies, but because of what they represented. Courage. Risk. Belief. Effort. Identity. Possibility. They taught me that stepping forward before you feel ready can sometimes be exactly what changes everything.

And sport was not the only place where I felt myself expanding.

Music was blooming in my life in a way I had not expected. At fourteen, I joined my older brother's band, *Stealing Time*. We played rock covers full of energy and attitude. Jimi Hendrix. Santana. Bob Marley. Songs that filled smoky pubs where noise was encouraged, and everyone felt larger than life.

I was the lead singer and guitarist, and I loved every second of it. The energy. The freedom. The permission to take up space without fear. I even slipped rum into my Coca Cola between sets, thinking I was clever, though I am sure the older guys knew exactly what I was doing.

Music gave me something sport could not.
A stage.
A spotlight.
A voice that did not stutter.
A confidence that did not hesitate.

Being surrounded by older musicians, including my brother, made me feel part of something powerful. We were a four piece band, and I brought modern influences to balance their classic rock tastes. Stray Cats. Duran Duran. Sharp beats. Catchy hooks. The blend worked. The crowds loved it. And playing alongside my brother felt like stepping into a world where age mattered less than presence and energy.

Sport was strengthening my body.
Music was strengthening my spirit.

Together, they were shaping my identity.

Beneath all that growing confidence, one truth remained. My stutter did not disappear. It still surfaced at unexpected moments. Speaking to certain teachers. Meeting new people. Being put on the spot. But this time, I did not let it shrink me.

Confidence does not erase difficulty.
It gives you the courage to move through it.

And I was learning how to do that every single day.

High school was chaotic and challenging.
But it was also where I began to understand my own potential.
The place where talent became opportunity.

Where opportunity became confidence.
And where confidence, slowly and steadily, became identity.

The world was getting bigger.

And this time, I was growing with it.

CHAPTER 2

Part 3: The Mindset Shift, the Growing
Confidence, and Finding Purpose in the Chaos

By the time I reached the middle years of high school, the world that
had once felt overwhelming began to feel manageable. Not easy. Not
comfortable. But familiar enough that I no longer felt like a small
boy wandering through a giant maze without a map. The corridors no
longer swallowed me whole. They became places I moved through
with purpose rather than anxiety. The faces around me were no
longer a blur of strangers. They became recognisable, predictable,
part of the background rhythm of daily life. Even the rules, though
still frustrating at times, began to make sense. I understood why they
existed, where they could be bent, and where they could not.

I had carved out a place for myself through effort, persistence, and a
quiet refusal to disappear.

That place was built piece by piece. Through rugby, where effort was
visible and respect was earned. Through athletics, where discipline
and repetition paid off over time. Through music, where confidence
flowed without hesitation. And through sheer stubborn
determination, the kind that grows when you realise no one is
coming to save you but yourself. Alongside all of that, a belief was
beginning to take shape inside me. A belief that I was capable of
more than anyone had expected, including myself. I no longer felt
like I was chasing confidence or trying to force it into existence. It
was slowly finding me, settling in naturally as I grew into it.

Confidence has a way of sneaking up on you. It does not arrive with
fanfare or announcements. It does not demand attention or declare
itself loudly. It shows up quietly, almost unnoticed, in moments you
only recognise in hindsight. In moments where you realise you are no
longer afraid to step forward. In moments where your body reacts

before your doubt has time to intervene. In moments where hesitation fades and action becomes instinct rather than effort.

I could feel that shift happening inside me, subtle but unmistakable.

The disruptive kid from my first year of high school had begun to grow up. Not completely. Not perfectly. But enough to recognise that my actions carried weight beyond myself. Enough to understand that behaviour had consequences, not just for me, but for the younger boys who watched how I moved, spoke, and reacted. Whether I liked it or not, I was being observed. The principal's words never left me. They stayed like a quiet echo in the background of my mind, surfacing whenever I felt myself drifting back toward old habits.

People look up to you.
Whether you realise it or not.
Act like someone worth looking up to.

Those words guided me more than I admitted at the time. I did not suddenly become a model student or a perfect example, but my choices began to shift. I started paying more attention in class, even when the subject did not immediately interest me. I listened more than I talked. I learned that silence could carry more strength than noise. I learned when to hold my tongue and when to speak up with intention. Discipline no longer felt like punishment imposed from the outside. It felt like alignment, like choosing a direction rather than being pushed into one.

Teachers noticed the change.
Classmates noticed it too.
And most importantly, I noticed it in myself.

With that shift came something unexpected. I began to enjoy learning.

Not every subject. Not every lesson. But certain classes began to pull me in. Maths started to make sense in a way it never had before. I found myself enjoying the logic of it, the structure, the way a problem could look impossible at first and then slowly unravel step by step until the answer revealed itself. Physics followed naturally. Movement, force, energy, cause and effect. It mirrored what I already understood through sport and motion. The world behaving according to rules, patterns, and principles you could observe, test, and prove.

Then there was art.

Art gave me something different again. A space where there was no single right answer. Where creativity mattered as much as technique. Where ideas could be expressed visually when words still sometimes failed me. Drawing, design, and visual thinking felt instinctive. It allowed me to translate thoughts into form without needing to explain them out loud. Looking back now, I can see how those three subjects together, maths, physics, and art, quietly carved a path that would only make sense much later in life. Logic. Systems. Creativity. Structure balanced with imagination. At the time, I simply followed what felt natural.

At first, the change was subtle.

I started handing assignments in on time without being chased. I noticed my marks slowly climbing. Concepts that once felt confusing began to click. I found myself participating instead of hiding. I felt a quiet sense of pride when teachers praised effort rather than talent. That mattered more to me than I realised at the time.

Before I knew it, my mindset toward school had shifted entirely. I was no longer just showing up out of obligation or routine. I was engaging. I was curious. I was learning. And the strange thing was, the more I learned, the more I wanted to learn. Knowledge stopped feeling like pressure and started feeling like possibility. It opened doors instead of closing them.

This academic growth did not replace sport. If anything, the two began to reinforce each other. Sport taught me discipline, focus, and resilience. Maths and physics sharpened my thinking. Art expanded how I saw the world. Together, they shaped a version of myself that finally felt whole. I realised I did not have to choose between being the athlete, the creative, or the student. I could be all of them at once.

Around this time, I began noticing how teachers treated older students differently. There was an unspoken respect, a sense of trust, an expectation of maturity. Sixth and seventh formers moved through the school with confidence and freedom. They were trusted with study periods. Trusted to manage their time. Trusted to behave like almost adults.

I wanted that.
I wanted to earn it.

And my behaviour began reflecting that desire more clearly each day.

At the same time, my social world was changing. I was no longer the shy boy lingering at the back of the room, hoping not to be noticed. My confidence around girls grew too. Not loud confidence. Not forced bravado. But something steadier and more natural. I could talk. Laugh. Joke. Relax. My stutter was still part of me, but it no longer controlled the moment. It might appear unexpectedly, but I did not let it dictate how I saw myself or how I showed up.

I was finally comfortable being seen.

Still, high school was not only about growth. It was also about temptation, missteps, and learning how to balance freedom with responsibility. There were moments where rebellion tugged at me again. Moments where I questioned whether school truly mattered. Moments where I wondered if there was another path waiting for me somewhere else.

That question grew louder when I started thinking about the army.

The idea appealed to me immediately. The structure. The discipline. The clear rules. The promise of direction. A clean break from uncertainty. A way out of complexity. A future that felt defined rather than open-ended.

But when I told my mother, everything erupted.

She fought it with everything she had. Not out of fear. Not out of control. But out of love.

Education comes first, she said.
You stay in sixth form.
Finish school.
Do not throw away your future.

She saw what I could not yet see. She saw possibility, opportunity, potential waiting just ahead. The argument was huge, the biggest we had ever had. Mum refused to back down. She refused to let me walk away from something I was only just beginning to build.

Then, in a moment that mixed desperation with strategy, she made a promise.

If you stay in school, I will buy you a motorbike from your brother.

She knew exactly what would reach me. And she was right.

Looking back now, I see it clearly. That moment was never really about a motorbike. It was about belief. My mother believed in a future I had not yet imagined for myself. Her insistence, her refusal to let me give up, became a turning point.

High school remained chaotic. Still demanding. Still overwhelming at times. But I was no longer stumbling through it blindly.

I was evolving.
Growing.
Becoming.

Slowly.
Steadily.
Deliberately.

And each step built momentum that would soon carry me into the next major chapter of my life. A chapter that would challenge everything I thought I knew about myself, about the world, and about how those early interests in logic, science, and creativity would one day converge and define the path ahead.

CHAPTER 2

Part 4: Sixth Form, Bill Sykes, and the
Realisation That Reinvention Was Already
Happening

By the time I reached sixth form, school no longer felt like
something I was reacting to. It felt like something I was stepping into
deliberately. The noise of the earlier years had quietened. The
uncertainty that once followed me from classroom to classroom had
eased. Even the fear that once sat in my chest when I spoke no longer
carried the same weight. A shift had taken place, not suddenly, but
gradually, the kind of change you only notice once you realise how
far you have come.

Sixth form felt like a threshold. Not a physical line you crossed, but a
mental one. The way people looked at you changed. Younger
students watched more closely. Teachers spoke with more directness
and trust. Expectations became less about rules and more about
responsibility. We were no longer sheltered by childhood, but not yet
fully released into adulthood. It was a space where choices mattered,
where direction started to form, and where effort carried real
consequences.

I felt ready for that shift. More prepared than I ever expected to feel.

This was the year my confidence began to move beyond
performance. It was no longer tied only to what I could do on a field
or on a stage. It settled into how I thought, how I listened, how I
responded. I trusted my judgement more. I questioned myself less. I
began to feel comfortable with the idea that I did not need to rush or
prove anything loudly. My direction was forming, even if I could not
yet fully articulate it.

Teachers treated us differently in sixth form, and that difference
mattered. They offered space instead of control. Choice instead of

instruction. They expected us to manage our time, own our outcomes, and learn from our mistakes. It was no longer about attendance or compliance. It was about engagement. And because they treated us like young adults, many of us rose to meet that expectation.

My relationships changed too. People who once felt distant or intimidating became familiar. Conversations deepened. Study groups formed naturally. Discipline became less about enforcement and more about intention. The habits I had built through training now showed up in my academic life. Planning made sense. Focus had purpose. Effort had visible return. The satisfaction of doing something properly began to matter as much in the classroom as it did anywhere else.

The more I committed, the more doors quietly opened.

Teachers noticed. Not in dramatic ways, but in how they invested time, encouragement, and challenge. When they saw consistency, they responded with trust. When they saw ability, they pushed further. When they saw leadership, they allowed space for it to grow. It was the first time I truly understood the influence educators could have when belief was paired with expectation. Learning stopped feeling like obligation and started to feel like leverage.

At the same time, the messages I had grown up hearing finally landed. My parents' voices carried weight now in a way they never had before. Staying in school. Building toward something better. Creating options instead of limits. For the first time, I was not pushing back against that guidance. I was choosing it.

Sport still played a central role in my life during that period. Rugby continued to ground me. Running remained a constant. Athletics sharpened my edge. Competing, representing teams, and stepping into leadership roles all contributed to a growing sense of capability.

But the moment that defined sixth form did not come from competition or training.

It came from the school musical.

Oliver.

Taking on the role of Bill Sykes demanded something entirely different from me. It required command, presence, control, and conviction. It required standing alone under lights, delivering lines clearly, singing, and holding the attention of an audience. For someone who had once struggled simply to introduce himself, it was a confrontation with everything that had ever made me doubt myself.

From the outside, it may have looked like just another performance. From the inside, it was a reckoning.

There was nowhere to hide. No movement to lean on. No physical outlet to mask uncertainty. I had to speak. I had to project. I had to occupy space fully and without apology. And I did.

The applause was secondary.
The achievement was internal.

That night changed how I saw myself. Not because the stutter disappeared, but because it no longer dictated what I could attempt. It became something I managed, not something that managed me. For the first time, I truly believed that the things which once limited me no longer defined the direction of my life.

Even so, sixth form was not free of challenge.

That was the year the idea of the army returned strongly. The appeal of structure, discipline, and purpose pulled at me. It felt clear. Direct. Honest. A way forward that did not require uncertainty. I could imagine myself there, training, testing limits, being shaped by order and challenge.

But my mother stood firm.

She challenged me harder than anyone else ever had. Not because she dismissed the army, but because she understood timing. She knew that walking away too early would close doors I had only just opened. Staying meant finishing sixth form. Finishing sixth form meant qualifications. Qualifications meant options. Options meant a future that extended far beyond what I could currently see.

We argued. Strongly. Emotionally. She refused to step aside. And in doing so, she held the line for a future I was not yet equipped to fight for myself.

In the end, I did not achieve University Entrance. But I completed sixth form, and that certificate proved to be enough. More than enough. It opened the door to my first career. A career that would take me across borders, industries, and experiences that reshaped my life in ways I never could have predicted.

As sixth form came to an end, something settled within me. A sense of completion. Pride. Readiness. And also a quiet sadness, knowing that the place which had tested, challenged, and shaped me was now behind me.

I did not leave high school as the boy who entered it.
I did not leave as the one who hid.
I did not leave as the one who disrupted.
I did not leave afraid of his own voice.

I left as someone prepared.
Someone grounded.
Someone curious.
Someone ready to take responsibility for his own direction.

The world waiting beyond Inglewood was larger, more demanding, and far less forgiving.
But it was also full of possibility.

And for the first time, I stepped toward it knowing I belonged there.

CHAPTER 3

Part 1: The Leap Into Adulthood and the First
Real Lessons of the World

Leaving high school felt like stepping out of a world that had shaped me and into one that offered no reassurance at all. The school gates closed behind me, and with them went the certainty of routine and the comfort of familiarity. Outside those gates, nothing paused to acknowledge what I had already lived through. There was no timetable telling me where to be. No bell setting the rhythm of my day. No teachers watching, guiding, correcting. No classmates to share laughter with in the small spaces between lessons. The responsibility landed all at once, and it felt both unsettling and strangely alive, like stepping out of warmth into sharp air that wakes you instantly.

That moment marked the real beginning.

I had not achieved University Entrance, but I had achieved enough. Enough to open a door. Enough to give me somewhere to start. For the first time, progress was no longer measured in grades or reports but in initiative and willingness. My mother's friend became the first person to point me toward a direction, suggesting telecommunications, an industry that at the time sat under the umbrella of the New Zealand Post Office. I did not yet understand what it truly involved. I had no grasp of how vast the field was or how deeply it would shape my future. I only knew it sounded technical, structured, and purposeful. It felt like work that mattered. Work that demanded concentration and accountability. Something about that resonated with me immediately.

I did not have a detailed plan. What I had instead was momentum, and momentum can often carry you further than clarity ever will.

I applied for an apprenticeship with New Zealand Telecom believing that effort and attitude would bridge any gaps. The interview quickly corrected that assumption. The General Manager was direct and honest. He explained that I was not at the top of the shortlist. Other candidates had stronger academic results, cleaner applications, and more impressive credentials. On paper, they were safer choices. His words were not cruel, but they were heavy, the kind that lodge themselves in your chest and stay there long after the conversation ends.

Yet even as he spoke, something inside me refused to accept that this was the end of the road.

It was a familiar feeling. The same quiet resistance that had surfaced whenever someone underestimated me or placed a ceiling on my potential. I did not argue. I did not plead. I did not try to explain who I was. Instead, I acted.

The next morning at eight o'clock, I returned to reception and asked politely if there had been any update. There had not. I thanked them and left. The following morning, I did the same. And the morning after that. For two full weeks, I arrived every day. Well dressed. Calm. Respectful. Determined. I did not demand answers. I did not complain. I did not push boundaries. I simply made it clear, through consistency alone, that I wanted the opportunity more than anyone else.

Slowly, I became a familiar face. Reception staff began greeting me by name. Some smiled. Some shook their heads in disbelief. Others asked quietly what I was hoping for. What none of them could ignore was that I kept coming back. I was learning something essential without even realising it at the time. Persistence, when paired with humility, communicates far more than words ever can.

Eventually, the General Manager called my mother. He told her that while my grades had not placed me first, my determination had shifted his perspective. He respected my consistency. He respected the fact that I refused to disappear quietly. Shortly after that conversation, the offer came through.

I got the apprenticeship.

Not because I looked best on paper.

But because I showed who I was through action.

That lesson stayed with me. It became a cornerstone of my adult life. Effort matters. Presence matters. Consistency builds trust where talent alone sometimes cannot. I would return to that lesson again and again, often without consciously realising it.

Stepping into working life felt different from anything I had experienced before. The expectations were clearer and less forgiving. If you did not turn up, there was no safety net. If you did not perform, the consequences were immediate. Responsibility was no longer theoretical. It was practical, daily, and unavoidable. I found that strangely comforting. There was honesty in it. You either showed up or you did not. You either learned or you stalled.

Sport remained deeply woven into my life during this period. Rugby continued to shape my weeks. Athletics kept my body sharp and my mind disciplined. But another influence began to grow alongside those pursuits. My older brother was deeply committed to bodybuilding. Watching him train with focus and intention fascinated me. He approached his body with respect and strategy. Every session had purpose. Every movement had meaning. Progress was measured over months and years, not days.

I joined the gym initially to become stronger for rugby. I wanted more power, more resilience, more control over my physical limits. What I discovered instead was a mindset that would stay with me long after sport itself evolved. The gym taught me structure. It taught me patience. It showed me how small, consistent effort compounds over time. It taught me to show up even when motivation was absent. To repeat movements until struggle gave way to mastery. To respect recovery as much as effort.

The discipline I built there did not stay confined to physical training. It flowed naturally into my work. Early mornings became manageable. Physical demands did not intimidate me. Fatigue felt familiar rather than overwhelming. Pressure no longer triggered panic. I knew how to push through discomfort without losing focus, because I had practiced doing exactly that day after day.

The gym, like sport, became another classroom. One without words or grades, but rich in lessons.

Outside of work, my life continued to expand. Friendships deepened. Social circles widened. Confidence in unfamiliar spaces grew steadily. I was no longer the boy shrinking back or hiding behind uncertainty. Conversations came more easily now. I could listen without anxiety. I could speak without rehearsing every sentence. My stutter still existed, but it no longer defined the moment. It appeared when it appeared, and I moved through it rather than around it.

I was growing into myself without trying to announce it.

Life felt full, but it never felt complete. There was a sense of momentum, but no illusion of arrival. The apprenticeship was only the beginning. I could feel that clearly. The adult world was layered and demanding in ways school never was. There were no pauses. No extensions. No allowances for potential. Only performance and reliability.

And yet, I felt ready.

Ready to learn more.
Ready to test myself.
Ready to see how far discipline, courage, and effort could carry me.

High school had shaped my character. Sport had shaped my resilience. Work was beginning to shape my purpose.

During these early working years, I began to truly understand the influence of my parents. Their work ethic. Their sacrifices. Their quiet insistence that nothing worth having comes without effort. Those lessons had embedded themselves in me long before I recognised them. Now they guided my standards, my decisions, and the way I approached every challenge placed in front of me.

I started to see how opportunity rarely arrives fully formed. It emerges gradually, often disguised as responsibility. It rewards those who show up consistently rather than those who wait to be noticed. The boy from Inglewood was becoming a man who understood direction. A man learning that consistency builds futures. That reliability creates trust. That humility keeps doors open long after talent stops impressing.

Looking back now, I see this period clearly. It was not merely a transition. It was a foundation. The first true step into the person I would become. The base layer beneath every reinvention, every challenge, and every chapter that followed.

The boy from Inglewood was no longer standing still.

He was moving.

He was learning how to trust the momentum created by discipline, effort, and belief.

And he was only just beginning to understand how far that momentum could take him.

CHAPTER 3

Part 2: The Apprenticeship That Built a Man

The first morning I walked into the New Zealand Post Office telecoms office, the air felt different from anything I had known at school. It carried weight. Not tension, not hostility, but purpose. The walls hummed softly with conversation, radios crackling, tools being moved from bench to bench. Coils of cable lay stacked neatly, copper glinting beneath their insulation. Older technicians moved through the space with unhurried confidence, men who understood systems so thoroughly they barely needed to speak about them. Everything here seemed to operate on precision, routine, and accountability.

I stood there in new boots that had not yet learned the shape of my feet, blue overalls stiff with fresh cotton, clutching a folder of documents filled with diagrams and terminology I barely understood. Pride rose alongside fear. School had been demanding, but this felt different. This was not a place where mistakes lived only on paper. Here, errors had consequences. A wrong connection could take down a business. A careless action could damage equipment worth more than my annual wage. A moment of laziness could ripple outward, slowing an entire team. This was the adult world, and its expectations pressed in on me before anyone even spoke my name.

Yet beneath the nerves, there was readiness. Or at least the belief that I could rise to what was required.

The first weeks of training dismantled any remaining illusions I had about ease. The pace was relentless. We were introduced to circuitry, cabling standards, switching principles, and network layouts that felt impossibly complex at first glance. Underground cable theory gave way to practical installation. Pole climbing safety led into live demonstrations. We learned how entire communities stayed connected through systems most people never considered until something failed.

The instructors were men shaped by decades of work. Their authority was quiet, rooted in experience rather than volume. Some had hands thickened and scarred by years of physical labour. Others carried a sharpness in their eyes that missed nothing. They did not waste words. They did not soften expectations. But they were fair. If you showed effort, they gave guidance. If you cut corners, they corrected you immediately.

They reminded me of the men I had watched growing up, those who gathered after long days of labour, sharing stories without exaggeration. Practical men. Skilled men. Builders of things that lasted. Standing among them made me feel small, but it also stirred something deeper. I wanted to earn my place. I wanted to carry myself with the same quiet assurance they had earned through years of showing up.

The first task seemed simple. Strip a section of cable cleanly, exposing the copper strands without damaging the insulation or weakening the internal wires. It looked straightforward. It was not. My first attempt went badly. I stripped too much, nicked the insulation, crushed one strand. The instructor gave a low chuckle and handed me another length.

Try again, he said. Nobody gets it right the first time.

I tried again. Then again. Then again. Each failure taught me something small. Pressure control. Patience. Awareness of feel rather than force. By the fifth attempt, frustration crept in. By the tenth, I produced a piece clean enough that the foreman gave a brief nod and moved on. That nod carried weight. It said more than praise ever could. It meant progress. It meant acceptance.

Training unfolded like that for months. Long days that left hands aching and uniforms stained. We climbed poles in all weather, learning balance and respect for height. We dug trenches through stubborn ground, discovering the value of steady effort. We crawled through ceilings thick with dust and heat, learning to work calmly in confined spaces. Slowly, the abstract became practical. Diagrams transformed into real connections. Theory took physical shape.

There was something powerful in understanding how the country functioned beneath the surface. Knowing how calls travelled. How signals moved. How infrastructure held everything together. It gave me a sense of contribution I had never felt before. This work mattered. People depended on it without ever seeing it.

But the systems were only part of the apprenticeship. The people shaped me just as much.

I worked alongside men from every background. Māori. Pākehā. Pacific Islanders. Young apprentices eager to prove themselves. Older technicians passing on knowledge without ceremony. Some filled the room with humour, stories spilling out as easily as breath. Others spoke rarely, but when they did, you listened. There were men who could diagnose faults instantly and others who took the long route but taught patience through methodical process.

I found myself drawn to those who treated me like a younger brother. Men who guided without condescension. Who understood my stutter without comment. Who offered advice through example rather than instruction. They reminded me of the uncles I had grown up around, men who carried wisdom in how they worked rather than how they spoke.

Every day brought lessons. Sometimes technical. Sometimes personal. Sometimes lessons about people. Sometimes lessons about myself. As the months passed, I realised how much of Inglewood I had carried into this place without realising it. The discipline forged through sport. The resilience shaped by managing my voice. The humility instilled by my parents. The courage learned in rivers and open spaces. The leadership developed through team sport. The grounding provided by whānau. All of it surfaced in how I showed up.

The apprenticeship also introduced pressures school could never simulate. Deadlines were real. Mistakes carried cost. Expectations were immediate. There were days when foremen pushed us hard, testing limits deliberately. Days when exhaustion pressed heavy. Days when wet trenches stretched endlessly. Days when errors embarrassed me deeply. Days when I questioned whether I had chosen the right path.

Yet quitting never entered my mind. Not once. I had fought for this opportunity. I had stood in reception for two weeks to earn my place. Once I had it, there was no walking away.

Pride became fuel. Pride in the uniform. Pride in responsibility. Pride in contributing to something larger than myself. Pride in knowing my parents saw me stepping into adulthood with purpose. Pride in proving to myself that I could operate in a world where hesitation had no room.

Outside of work, life demanded balance. Rugby still consumed my weekends. Training filled evenings. Work demanded physical output every day. The strain was real, but it sharpened me. Time management emerged not as a concept but as necessity. Discipline stopped being optional. Endurance expanded beyond muscle into mindset.

During this period, my relationship with my girlfriend deepened, as did my connection to her family. Her father became an unexpected mentor. He carried himself with calm authority. His words were measured. His presence steady. Conversations with him encouraged reflection rather than reaction. He showed me that strength did not need to announce itself. That control came from understanding rather than dominance. That manhood was as much about restraint as it was about action.

Spending time with him shaped how I viewed responsibility and emotional maturity. The bond we formed endured long after circumstances changed. To this day, whenever I return to New Zealand, I still visit them. That connection remains part of my foundation.

The apprenticeship shaped me on multiple levels. Technically, it gave me language and systems thinking. Physically, it built resilience and endurance. Socially, it expanded my understanding of people. Spiritually, it grounded me in purpose.

Those years were not glamorous. There were no applause moments. No public recognition. But they built something lasting. They formed habits I would rely on for decades. They instilled standards I would not compromise. They prepared me for complexity long before I encountered it.

By the time I completed my apprenticeship, I was not just qualified. I was changed. I carried confidence earned through consistency. I understood responsibility through experience. I trusted my ability to learn under pressure.

The next chapter waited beyond those years. A chapter that would take me far beyond New Zealand, deeper into global systems, and further into my own potential. But before that journey began, there was a pivot. A decision that would redirect everything.

The foundation had been laid.

What came next would test it completely.

And I did not yet know how much I would need everything I had learned to survive what was ahead.

CHAPTER 3

Part 3: The whisper that became a War cry

Finishing the apprenticeship should have felt like reaching a summit. Three years of learning, training, sweating, failing, adjusting, and finally becoming a fully fledged technician. A tradesman. A professional. A young Māori (Indigenous person of New Zealand) man holding a qualification that promised stability, respect, and opportunity. People congratulated me. My parents were proud in that quiet way that meant more than celebration. My management shook my hand firmly, their nod carrying an unspoken acknowledgement that I had earned my place.

Yet when I stood there with the certificate in my hands, I felt no sense of arrival. Instead, I felt like I had only just reached the base of something much larger. The view ahead was not clarity but scale. I could see how much more there was to learn, how much responsibility came with competence, and how small my experience still was in the context of the wider world.

Completing the apprenticeship was not an ending. It was permission to begin.

The safety net vanished almost immediately. There were no instructors double checking my work. No fellow apprentices learning alongside me. No shared uncertainty. Suddenly, it was just me. Me climbing poles in unpredictable weather. Me diagnosing faults while customers hovered anxiously. Me being accountable for outcomes without explanation or excuse. In the real world, mistakes did not become learning exercises. They became disruptions. Costs. Delays. Frustration. And so I learned to move with intention. I learned when to slow down. When to trust experience. When to pause and reassess rather than rush toward an answer.

Responsibility reshaped how I thought. Precision became instinctive. Adaptability became necessary. Confidence became quiet and internal rather than something displayed.

The work took me across Taranaki and beyond. Each job brought new environments, new systems, new expectations. I worked in family homes where a phone line was the only link to the outside world. I worked in businesses where downtime meant lost revenue. I worked in government buildings where standards were strict and scrutiny high. Each site demanded professionalism, clarity, and respect.

Along the way, I partnered with senior technicians whose experience dwarfed my own. Men who had seen technologies rise and fall. Who understood not only how systems worked, but why they were built the way they were. Some taught patiently, breaking down complexity into understandable pieces. Others were gruff and unsentimental, expecting you to keep up or fall behind. From each, I learned something valuable. Technique. Judgment. Perspective.

I absorbed everything. Not just what was said, but how it was said. Not just what was done, but why it was done that way.

During this period, I discovered something important about how my mind worked. Telecoms was technical, but it was also intuitive. Fault finding required more than following procedures. It demanded pattern recognition. The ability to sense inconsistencies. To notice behaviour in systems that did not quite align. I found myself tracing problems not only with logic but with feel. I could often predict where an issue lay before fully articulating why.

At the time, I thought this was simply part of the trade. Only much later did I realise that this way of thinking would become one of my defining strengths in far more complex environments.

Life beyond work continued to expand. Rugby remained central, anchoring me physically and socially. As my confidence grew in my professional life, it translated naturally onto the field. Responsibility at work sharpened my sense of accountability in sport. Training felt purposeful. Matches carried weight. Rugby kept me connected to community and discipline in ways nothing else could.

Surfing, too, deepened into something more meaningful. It was no longer just a pastime. It became ritual. Release. A way to strip away the noise that accumulated during the week. My best mate and I chased waves whenever we could, travelling the coast in search of breaks that tested us. Raglan offered rhythm and flow. Wellington demanded adaptability. The Surf Highway delivered consistency and challenge through places that felt almost sacred.

Hours spent in the water taught me lessons I carried everywhere else. Patience mattered. Timing mattered. Respect for forces beyond your control mattered. Panic made everything worse. Calm opened options. Persistence created opportunity. Surfing became a mirror for how I approached work, relationships, and ambition.

Despite the stability forming around me, something new began to stir. Not dissatisfaction. Not boredom. Something quieter. A restlessness rooted in curiosity. Stories from travellers passed through my awareness like sparks. Conversations about Europe, America, Asia lingered long after they ended. Photographs of distant cities triggered a tightening in my chest, a sense that my world was larger than the map I had known so far.

I loved my job. I valued my community. My whānau (extended family) grounded me. But my instinct had always been to test boundaries. To step forward rather than settle. Every phase of my life had been defined by movement into the unknown. This felt no different. The idea of travelling overseas did not feel reckless. It felt aligned.

Still, leaving was not an easy decision. It meant stepping away from security. From routine. From belonging. From the people who had shaped me. It meant trading certainty for possibility.

I began saving quietly. Methodically. Each dollar had intention. I did not announce the plan because I needed to live with it first. Sometimes speaking a dream aloud invites doubt too early. I wanted to feel the decision settle internally before it became public.

My girlfriend sensed the shift long before I voiced it. We talked late into the night, unpacking excitement and fear in equal measure. She understood the pull even when it scared her. Her father encouraged me in the same grounded way he had always guided me. He recognised that growth often demands distance.

Their support steadied me. It affirmed that this was not escape. It was expansion.

I worked harder than ever during that period. Extra shifts. More responsibility. Saving relentlessly. Every long day felt purposeful. The restlessness transformed into anticipation. Travel was no longer an idea. It became intention.

At twenty three, I committed. I would leave. I would travel. I would give myself two years to see the world.

Booking the flights marked a psychological shift. A clear dividing line between who I had been and who I was becoming. I was choosing uncertainty deliberately. Not because I lacked direction, but because I trusted my ability to adapt.

As departure approached, life sharpened. Time with friends felt richer. Workdays carried weight. Moments with my girlfriend's family felt precious. Runs along the coast became reflective. Surf sessions stretched longer. Final gatherings with whānau (extended family) were heavy with unspoken emotion.

The day I boarded the plane, I carried my past with me. Inglewood. School. Sport. Apprenticeship. Family. All of it travelled quietly inside me.

I was no longer just a young man from a small town.

I was a young man stepping into the world.

And I had no understanding yet of how deeply that step would reshape everything I thought I knew about myself, about others, and about what was possible.

The foundation had been laid.

The next transformation was about to begin.

CHAPTER 3

When the plane lifted off from New Zealand soil, I felt something inside me lift as well. It was not relief and it was not freedom in the way people often describe it. It was something deeper and harder to name. Something like expansion. Like my chest opening and my lungs finally taking in a fuller breath. I sat by the window watching the land I knew so well shrink beneath layers of cloud that felt indifferent to my story. The mountains, the rivers, the towns that had shaped me disappeared quietly. And although fear was tucked somewhere inside me, it was outweighed by anticipation. I was stepping into the unknown carrying nothing more than a backpack, a handful of contacts, and a confidence forged slowly over years of effort, resilience, and learning how to back myself without applause.

My first stop was Los Angeles. I had imagined it for years in fragments and fantasies, built from films, television, and stories passed between young people dreaming of places far away. The reality hit me immediately. The heat wrapped around me before I even cleared the terminal. The noise followed close behind. Traffic, voices, music, movement, life operating at a volume that made New Zealand feel like a quiet murmur. I felt conspicuously out of place and strangely energised at the same time. Anonymous. Unnoticed. Alive.

The weeks that followed tested me in ways no apprenticeship ever could. There were no familiar systems to lean on. I navigated bus routes without knowing the suburbs or their reputations. I learned how to stretch money across days, sometimes meals. I figured out how to blend into streets where nobody knew my name or cared to ask. At first it was overwhelming, but slowly I found my rhythm. I learned to ask questions without hesitation. To trust strangers just enough. To take risks without paralysis. I discovered that I could adapt far quicker than I ever gave myself credit for.

But Los Angeles was only the threshold.

Europe was the destination pulling at me with real force.

When I finally landed in London, the shift was immediate. The air felt heavier. Colder. Older. The city carried history in its bricks, its streets, the way people moved with purpose shaped by centuries before them. I had friends living in East Grinstead, and they welcomed me with generosity that softened the landing more than I can properly express. What began as a couch became a room, then a home, then a sense of belonging that made the early months overseas feel possible. Those friendships deepened into bonds that have lasted decades.

East Grinstead became my base. A small English town with its own rhythm, humour, and quiet strength. Pubs with low ceilings and dark wood. Streets that felt untouched by time. Shops that seemed to exist in a different century. It was a place where I learned how to stand inside a foreign culture without erasing myself. How to adapt without disappearing.

But I did not cross the world to stay still.

I was there to work.

To learn.

To stretch myself.

To chase something larger than familiarity.

Even while travelling, even while building a career, the connection to home never faded. It surfaced unexpectedly. In a song drifting through a pub. In a smell from a street vendor. In the sound of a Māori (Indigenous person of New Zealand) accent overheard in a London market. Small reminders that grounded me in who I was and where I came from. The longer I stayed overseas, the stronger those echoes became.

Then I met the woman who would become my wife. That changed everything.

We built our life in increments. A shared flat. Shared responsibilities. Shared dreams spoken quietly at night. I began to settle in ways I had not anticipated. The world was still wide and demanding, but now it was shaping the foundation of a family rather than just my ambition.

When our two children arrived, something fundamental shifted inside me. Travel remained part of my work, but it was no longer driven by restlessness. It was driven by purpose. My focus sharpened. My decisions became more deliberate. My ambition gained structure. The stakes were no longer abstract. Responsibility had faces. Names. Futures.

For the first time in my life, my purpose was not centred on me. It was centred on them. And then life tested me.

The test came during an economic storm that would be remembered for generations. Black Wednesday. Mortgage rates in the UK surged past fourteen percent. Businesses trembled. Industries contracted. Jobs disappeared overnight. I felt the impact immediately. My role was made redundant. When I was told, it felt like the floor gave way beneath me. Losing a job when you are young carries one weight. Losing it when you have a family, a mortgage, and responsibility carries another entirely.

Fear surfaced briefly. Then it was gone. It was not allowed to stay.

I had built too much resilience, too much capability, to be undone by a single blow. I had skills. I had instincts. And I had people depending on me. So I moved forward.

I contacted everyone I knew. Vendors. Engineers. Managers. Suppliers. People I had helped. People who trusted my work ethic and my ability to deliver under pressure. Consulting and contracting were not career moves at first. They were survival. But they became something much bigger.

The next ten years were the most intense period of technical growth I had ever experienced. I carved out a reputation as a specialist. Someone who understood complex systems. Someone who could step into chaos and extract solutions. Someone who remained steady when pressure peaked. Clients began requesting me by name.

I found my way into digital telecommunications at exactly the right moment. The telecom boom. Government deregulation. The timing was perfect. The 1980s and early 1990s were defined by transformation. Networks expanded rapidly. Microwave transmission and enterprise infrastructure became essential. Systems evolved faster than companies could adapt. The foundations I had built in New Zealand suddenly unlocked opportunities across Europe.

I stepped into work far beyond anything I had known. Roles that demanded precision, depth, and speed. I studied relentlessly. Enrolled in courses. Attended vendor certifications, often funded by companies who saw my potential. The apprenticeship that once felt substantial now felt like an introduction.

I learned quickly.
I adapted quickly.
I moved quickly.
The industry did not wait.

I travelled constantly for work. Not holidays. Assignments. Contracts. High stakes troubleshooting. Germany. Norway. Sweden. France. The Netherlands. Spain. Denmark. Each country carried its own systems, expectations, and challenges. Airports became routine.

Hotels blurred together. I spent more time solving problems than unpacking bags.

Telecom companies sought specialists who understood emerging systems and the complexities of SS7 protocol. The signalling backbone of digital networks. Call setup. Routing. Charging. The invisible system holding everything together. I did not just understand it technically. I understood it intuitively.

I became the person called when systems failed and time mattered.

From Europe, my work extended further. I was flown from Norway to Saudi Arabia for specialised consulting. Saudi was confronting at first. The heat. The formality. The intensity. But it also refined me. The stakes were higher. The expectations uncompromising. The systems enormous. And there I was, a Māori (Indigenous person of New Zealand) man from Inglewood, working inside high security facilities solving problems entire teams had failed to resolve.

It was surreal.
Intimidating.
Exhilarating.

Saudi taught me discipline at a different level. Precision mattered. Respect mattered. Punctuality mattered. There were no shortcuts. No improvisation. Long days. Limited freedom. Sometimes the outside world existed only through tinted windows between site and accommodation. Yet I thrived. The local engineers invited me to eat with them, asked about my culture, shared theirs with me. In those moments, connection crossed borders effortlessly.

I saw parts of the world I never imagined. I learned how to communicate across language, culture, and expectation. I began seeing myself differently. In New Zealand, I had been the boy who stuttered.

The runner.
The sports kid.
The hard worker from Inglewood.

In Europe and the Middle East, I was the expert. The specialist. The one flown in to fix what others could not.

The moment it truly landed came late one night in a Norwegian control room. A system failure. Tension heavy in the air. Engineers waiting behind me. I traced a pattern no one else had seen. Followed instinct. Found a deeply buried configuration fault.

When the system came back online, the room shifted. Relief became respect. Doubt became trust. And I understood something fundamental. I belonged in the world. Not just at home. Not just where I was known. But anywhere skill, discipline, and courage were valued.

Years of pressure, travel, and complexity shaped me into someone stronger than I had imagined. Yet with every country crossed and every system repaired, I felt another shift beginning.

Something bigger was approaching. Something personal. Something that would test me beyond technology. The next chapter was already forming. And I was moving toward it faster than I realised.

CHAPTER 3

Part 5: Where Curiosity Because Destiny

As I look back on that period now, I can see that my personal growth was unfolding alongside one of the most significant technological shifts of the modern era. The telecommunications boom was not a passing trend or a burst of new ideas. It was a structural transformation that changed how the world connected, communicated, and functioned. Those years became a crossroads, not only in my own life, but for a whole generation of engineers learning to operate in a world moving faster than anyone had been prepared for.

Telecommunications began shedding its old skin. What had once been slow, rigid, and centrally controlled evolved into systems that were faster, more modular, and increasingly digital. Analogue switching gave way to digital platforms capable of handling greater volumes with greater reliability. Copper networks, once the backbone of communication, were stretched close to their limits. Mobile infrastructure expanded at speed, changing not just how people spoke, but what they expected from being connected. Signalling systems like SS7 became the unseen nervous system of global connectivity, quietly managing call routing, billing, and control across borders. Voice, data, and signalling, once separate disciplines, merged into a single, interdependent ecosystem that demanded a new way of thinking.

That convergence changed everything.
And it changed what it meant to be an engineer.

In earlier decades, engineers often joined a company and stayed there for life. Careers unfolded slowly. Knowledge was guarded and passed down carefully. Systems evolved in measured steps. Stability mattered more than speed. But digital telecommunications disrupted that model. Innovation moved quicker than internal teams could absorb it. Networks became more interconnected, more critical, and more complex. Organisations could no longer wait for experience to accumulate over decades. Expertise had to move, and the people who could move with it became valuable.

That is why many of us shifted into contracting and consulting, not chasing freedom for its own sake, but because the industry demanded flexibility. Companies needed specialists who could arrive quickly, understand unfamiliar environments, stabilise systems, share knowledge, and deliver under pressure. Experience became currency. Adaptability became essential. Learning stopped being a phase and became a permanent state, driven by urgency and responsibility rather than comfort.

Learning digital telecommunications during that boom felt like standing in the centre of something unstoppable. Every new network deployment quietly reshaped everyday life. Calls became clearer. Connections became faster. Distance mattered less. What once required hours, days, or physical presence began happening in seconds. Most people never saw the work behind it, but engineers were building invisible highways that would soon carry far more than voice. We were laying foundations for a connected world that had not yet found its name.

We could feel the future approaching before it fully arrived.

Mobile phones were shrinking while their capability grew. Early data services hinted at a time when information would travel everywhere with you instead of living in offices, filing cabinets, or libraries. Gadgets were no longer simple tools. They were becoming extensions of how people organised their lives, relationships, and work. Communication shifted from something planned and deliberate to something constant and immediate. Digital telecommunications became the base layer beneath everything that followed: smartphones, messaging platforms, video conferencing, streaming, remote work, and global collaboration.

At the time, nobody spoke about digital transformation the way people do now. We were too busy building it. We learned on live networks where mistakes carried consequences. We fixed problems in real time. We watched systems evolve while customers depended on them, often unaware of how fragile or complex the machinery beneath their daily calls really was. Success was immediate. Failure was visible. The learning curve was unforgiving, but it forged engineers who could see patterns, dependencies, and systems rather than isolated components.

The shift toward contracting and consulting revealed a deeper truth about knowledge itself. Expertise no longer lived in buildings, job titles, or hierarchies. It lived in people. The most effective engineers were not those who memorised documentation, but those who could walk into chaos, recognise patterns, understand the flow of traffic and signalling, and restore order under pressure. That skill travelled well. It crossed organisational boundaries, national borders, and cultural differences without needing translation.

Digital telecommunications did far more than reshape careers. It reshaped society.

It changed how families stayed connected across oceans. How businesses operated across time zones. How emergency services coordinated responses. How governments communicated with citizens. It laid the groundwork for a world where devices would speak to each other, where data would move faster than people, and where technology would be woven so deeply into daily life that it would eventually become invisible.

Looking back, I realise how fortunate I was to learn during that era. Not because it was easy, but because it demanded constant growth. It forced engineers to evolve alongside the technology rather than lag behind it. It rewarded curiosity over certainty, humility over ego, and movement over comfort. It taught us that staying relevant meant staying open.

That period did not just teach me how networks worked.
It taught me how the world works when connection becomes constant.

Without fully realising it at the time, it planted seeds of questions that would follow me much later. Questions about scale. About human impact. About responsibility. About how technology should support people rather than overwhelm them. Questions that would eventually pull me toward building, creating, and shaping systems beyond telecommunications. The boom was more than a chapter in my career. It was a preview of what was coming, a future defined by connected devices, intelligent systems, and a world where communication would no longer be a privilege, but an expectation.

But beneath all of that momentum, something else was building. Something quieter. A kind of inner transformation that did not announce itself loudly, but settled gradually, like the slow rise of the tide.

The first real shift happened in Europe, during a long train ride between assignments. I remember staring out the window at fields stretching into the horizon and realising that, for the first time, my thoughts were not locked on pressure, performance, or the next technical demand. I was thinking about meaning. About direction. About the shape of my life. I was no longer living only day to day. I was beginning to imagine a future that felt bigger and more intentional.

Those years built a professional backbone that would support every chapter to come. I moved through companies, contracts, and countries. I worked alongside executives, engineers, startups, and long-established incumbents. I learned how telecom infrastructure evolved through innovation and necessity. I learned how to navigate commercial pressure, operational failures, political decisions, and financial constraints.

But life was not done testing me.

Another economic slowdown arrived, and this time the loss was not only financial. It was personal. Divorce entered my life like a storm that no one predicts even when the clouds are visible. It was emotionally devastating. It stripped me in ways no job loss ever could. It forced me to confront parts of myself I had never examined, the proud parts, the vulnerable parts, the parts still holding old patterns from boyhood and early adulthood.

It was one of the hardest periods of my life.
And yet, the pain carried its own strange clarity.

Survival became a mantra.
Growth became a necessity.
Resilience became armour.

Every obstacle I had overcome up to that point, childhood challenges, speech struggles, restless years, the grind of early work, the pressure of overseas consulting, suddenly made sense. It had all been preparation. It had built the internal structure necessary to survive the collapse of a life I once believed was permanent.

A simple thought kept me moving:
If I have survived everything before this, I can survive this too.

And I did.
Not quickly.
Not easily.
But steadily.

I rebuilt my life piece by piece. I rebuilt my confidence. I rebuilt my career. And I rebuilt the man I wanted to be, for myself and for my children. What emerged from those years was a stronger version of me. Not polished. Not perfect. But aware. Grounded. Open. Determined.

It was this version of me that eventually stepped into a new long-term role, one that would define the next chapter of my career and shape nearly two decades of my life. A nineteen-year tenure with a respected telecommunications company. A role where I evolved from technician into design engineer, contributed to RFPs, worked alongside CTOs, directors and head of departments, designed infrastructure that supported millions, and collaborated with teams who became like extended whānau (family).

Those years gave me stability.
They gave me pride.
They gave me mastery.
And they gave me the space to dream again.

Because even after building a solid career and surviving what could have broken me, something inside me began to move once more. A quiet whisper. A sense of calling. A feeling that the next reinvention was coming. The world had shaped me. Telecoms had matured me. Travel had broadened me. Fatherhood had deepened me. Pain had refined me.

There are chapters in a man's life where the outside world assumes nothing significant is happening because everything looks calm, predictable, and steady. But on the inside, something deeper is shifting. Something invisible. Like standing on the shoreline at low tide, knowing the ocean is gathering itself quietly, preparing a wave no one else can see yet.

This was that chapter for me.

My days moved in patterns I could predict: early commutes, technical meetings, architecture diagrams, project deadlines, Friday afternoon laughs in the office kitchen, alternate weekends with my children, rugby on TV, familiar conversations with friends, the comforting rhythm of routine. It should have felt like I had arrived. I had stability. I had a respected role. I had a reputation earned through years of work. I had balance in ways I once thought impossible.

But beneath all of that, something in me began to vibrate at a different frequency. Not loud enough to disrupt my life, but steady enough that I could feel it even when I wasn't paying attention. A sense that something bigger was waiting. That a chapter I had not yet imagined was forming on the horizon. That purpose was reshaping itself quietly, preparing to reveal its next direction when the time was right.

I did not talk about this feeling.
Not to colleagues.
Not to family.
Not to friends.

It wasn't a crisis.
It wasn't boredom.
It wasn't dissatisfaction.

It was evolution.

A gentle, almost spiritual unfolding that happens when you have lived enough life to understand that stability is not the finish line. It is the foundation for building something greater.

Around this time, telecommunications entered another phase. Systems accelerated toward digital transformation. Businesses shifted from legacy infrastructure toward cloud-based environments. The early seeds of automation began to sprout. Teams were still manually doing tasks that machines could handle faster. Paperwork piled up. Leaders were overwhelmed by the pace of change. Customers wanted faster, smarter service, and many companies struggled to deliver.

I watched all of it with a clarity I did not yet know would matter. I watched from the inside. From the edges. From the perspective of someone who had seen systems across continents. And slowly, questions began to rise, not technical questions, but human ones.

How were people going to cope with this speed?
How would businesses survive without evolving?
How would teams work smarter, not harder?
How would leaders adapt to automation they didn't understand?
Where were the tools that could bridge the gap between human capacity and technological growth?

These questions were not about engineering.
They were about the future.

Fear of change is powerful.
It freezes people in place.
It convinces them survival is safer than evolution.
It keeps them rooted in systems that quietly drain them.

But I wasn't built that way.

My life had been one long lesson in adaptation. Constant movement. Constant change. Constant learning. I had shifted countries, roles, responsibilities, and mindsets. I had rebuilt after divorce. I had learned stability after storms. I had taught myself to adapt faster than circumstances changed. This instinct would eventually become the foundation of everything I built, though at the time it was simply a whisper that kept returning: you're not done yet.

That whisper grew stronger when I noticed something new in myself. I was no longer interested only in doing the work. I was interested in how the work could evolve. How systems could be improved. How processes could be redesigned. How technology could empower people instead of overwhelm them.

The technical world teaches you discipline.
Fatherhood teaches you compassion.
Life experience teaches you perspective.
But purpose teaches you direction.

And I could feel direction returning, not through dramatic moments, but through small realisations and quiet clarity, by noticing patterns others overlooked. It came during late-night changes at home. In the hum of servers. In the glow of screens. In the silence between deadlines. In the long walk to the station after solving a pain point with a solution. In the deep breath after presenting designs to executives. In the steady awareness that the world was shifting faster each year.

Those moments became the building blocks of what would eventually become my entrepreneurial identity. Not born from ego. Not born from ambition. Born from noticing what others did not see. Born from sensing where the world was heading. Born from understanding the need before the market even recognised it.

At the same time, my connection to culture deepened. Perhaps because reflection was becoming more frequent. Perhaps because identity matters differently as you move through manhood. Perhaps because I wanted to understand myself more fully as a Māori man raising children in a world that does not always nurture cultural grounding.

I read more about whakapapa.
I returned to the teachings of whānau.
I thought about Inglewood, the rivers, the unity, the laughter, the people who shaped me.
I thought about how far I had travelled and how many I carried with me in spirit each time I stepped into a new space.
I realised how much the lessons from elders, the mistakes, the humility, the respect, the perseverance, had guided me without me always noticing.

Cultural grounding is not something you perform.
It is something you embody.
Something you carry.
Something that shapes how you lead, how you listen, how you serve, and how you build.

It kept my perspective wide when environments tried to narrow it.
It kept my ego low when praise tried to inflate it.
It kept ambition honest when success tried to rush me.
It kept my heart steady when challenges tried to knock me off balance.

All of it, the reflection, the shifts, the questions, the internal widening, led to a deeper truth.

A new chapter was coming.

One that would require everything I had learned.
Everything I had lived.
Everything I had endured.

I didn't know its name yet. I didn't know its shape or timing. But I could feel it building quietly, patiently, relentlessly, like the tide rising under a still surface, like a wave forming beyond the horizon.

And I knew one thing for certain:
When the moment came, I would be ready.

All of it was preparing the man I would become next.
A founder.
A creator.
A builder of something new.

But that story was waiting in the chapters ahead. For now, the man who once climbed poles in Taranaki had crossed worlds, learned through fire, rebuilt through struggle, and discovered again and again that reinvention was not only possible, it was necessary.

The journey was far from over.
It was only evolving.

CHAPTER 4

Part 1: The Seed That Started The Journey

Even after everything I've accomplished, the wins, the losses, the
battles I've had to fight quietly, the sacrifices no one ever sees, I've
always had this nagging feeling deep in my chest that I'm not done
yet. That my best contribution is still ahead of me, waiting
somewhere just past the next corner. Māori (Indigenous people of
New Zealand) call it wairua (spirit or inner guiding essence), that
inner voice, that guiding presence. Some describe it as intuition,
others as purpose tapping you on the shoulder. For me, it has always
been a familiar whisper, sometimes gentle, sometimes relentless,
reminding me that my journey isn't finished.

That whisper became a roar the year I joined a new golf club.
I had been looking forward to it like a kid waiting to open presents
on Christmas morning. New course, new routines, new people, all
the bits of life that keep us growing. I imagined myself joining a 2-
ball or 3-ball group, talking rubbish with the boys, maybe arguing
over who had the better swing (spoiler: not me). But round after
round, I found myself walking that course alone.

Now, I'm an outgoing bloke. I've lived enough life to know that the
worst someone can say is "no," and even then, you're still standing.
So walking up to people and asking if I could join their game didn't
bother me. But it struck me that it might bother someone else. A lot
of people, actually. Not everyone has the confidence to walk into a
club where they know no one, put themselves out there, or risk
feeling unwelcome. Some people carry anxiety, self-doubt, or
memories of exclusion from earlier in life, memories that cling like
burrs on your socks.

Standing on that fairway one afternoon, I realised something
important: loneliness wasn't about the lack of people around you; it

was about the lack of connection. And in that moment, something inside me clicked.

I remember thinking, There has to be a better way. A way to connect people who want to play, exercise, compete, or just belong.

That was the seed. A tiny idea. A quiet voice.

And if life has taught me anything, it's this:
When something keeps returning to you listen.
Because that's purpose trying to get your attention.

At first, the idea felt like one of those random thoughts you get in the shower, good at the time but gone by lunchtime. But this one didn't go away. It followed me into the car, into the office, onto the course, and into the evenings while I was trying to relax. It was like one of those cheeky cousins at a whānau (extended family) gathering who sits next to you and keeps elbowing you in the ribs until you finally turn and ask what they want.

Eventually, I realised it wasn't a nuisance, it was a calling.

And when a calling shows up, you either answer it or spend the rest of your life wondering what might have been.

So I started talking. Not pitching, not planning, just talking. Sharing the idea with a close friend during late-night chats over a few pints. It became a ritual, really. We both lived through enough storms to recognise when someone was onto something.

"So you're 60... and you want to build a mobile app?"
He said it half-jokingly, half-concerned I'd finally lost the plot.

But once the laughter settled, something interesting happened:
He leaned in.

He asked questions.
He saw what I saw.

That's how Glluz Sports Mobile App was born, not as a business idea, but as a solution to a human problem.

I wanted to help people find connection. That's the heart of it. Not revenue. Not downloads. Not some flashy tech unicorn dream. Connection. Whanaungatanga (relationships and sense of belonging). Belonging.

And when your motivation comes from service, from building something for people who need it, you're fuelled by a different kind of fire.

I'd love to say I had it all figured out. That I had some grand roadmap, or years of experience in the mobile app world. But the truth is, I had absolutely no idea where to start. None. Zero.

I had a 30-year engineering background, telecoms, networks, voice architecture, but mobile apps? That felt like walking into a gym for the first time and pretending you knew how every machine worked. A part of me felt like an imposter. A bigger part of me felt like a beginner. And another part of me, the Māori (Indigenous person of New Zealand) part reminded me of who I come from.

I am the son of a Ngāti Porou (tribe from the East Coast of New Zealand) father, born into a large whānau (extended family) from the East Coast, raised among people who didn't break under pressure but bent like supplejack and sprang back even stronger. I grew up hearing stories about my maori (Māori Indigenous) grandfather, I met him when I was young but only faint and misted images, but most of what shaped my image of him came from others. A man of quiet mana (authority, prestige, spiritual power), strong values, and that typical East Coast stubbornness that I very clearly inherited.

My great-grandfather English, another thread woven into this long, messy, beautiful braid of identity. And then on the other side, my mother, Ngā Puhi (tribe from Northland, New Zealand) fierce, intelligent, unapologetic, and strong enough to walk into Taranaki. She showed resilience, empathy, and respect.

All these people live inside me. Their choices, their courage, their survival.

So yes, I didn't know the mobile app world.
But I knew how to:
solve problems
push through overwhelm
learn fast
figure things out
keep moving when others stop
ask for help when I need it
stand tall in rooms where I didn't yet belong

That's whakapapa (genealogy, lineage).
That's Māori (Indigenous people of New Zealand) resilience.
That's the inheritance no one can ever take away.

Once I committed to Glluz, the next step seemed simple:
Find a developer.

Except nothing is ever that simple.

I put some feelers out. Spoke to a few people. Looked online. And suddenly, it was like every developer, agency, freelancer and their dog wanted to work with me. Messages everywhere. Proposals. Recommendations. Offers. Prices ranging from the suspiciously cheap to the "are you building me an app or buying me a small country?" expensive.

It was overwhelming, but a good kind of overwhelming. Because beneath the chaos, I recognised something familiar: the discovery and execution process.

Telecom engineering teaches you discipline.
It teaches you to trust the blueprint, even when you can't yet see the finished product.
It teaches you that the right mindset is worth more than the right tools.

And so I trusted myself.

I reminded myself that I'd built systems more complex than most people ever see.
That I'd been responsible for infrastructures serving millions.
That I had navigated corporate storms, restructures, mergers, pressure, and expectations most people would crumble under.

I didn't know mobile apps, but I wasn't starting from nothing.

When I shared my plans at home, my wife didn't flinch. She didn't laugh. She didn't question me. She backed me completely. Not with blind optimism, but with belief. Genuine belief.

That was the moment I knew I wasn't chasing a hobby. I was stepping into a new chapter of my life.

As I continued refining the idea, something shifted. I realised Glluz wasn't just about sports. It wasn't just about golf, or football, or running groups.
It was about belonging.

Humans need connection the way lungs need air.
We're not built to walk through life alone.

I thought about people who had moved to a new city or country.
People who had struggled with confidence.
People who had experienced social anxiety.
People who had lost touch with old friends.
People who were older and didn't know where to meet others anymore.
People who wanted to get fit but didn't know where to begin.
People from cultural backgrounds where walking into a new space didn't always feel safe or welcomed.

I thought about Māori (Indigenous people of New Zealand) men in particular, our struggle with isolation, mental health, pride, and silence. How many of us bottle things up because we don't have the right environment to talk, to connect, to feel comfortable being ourselves.

What if an app could change that?
What if technology could bring people together instead of pulling them apart?

Suddenly, Glluz felt bigger than me.
It felt bigger than golf.
It felt like something that could genuinely help people.

There's a strange thing that happens when you hit a certain age.
Society starts whispering little lies into your ear:
"You're past it."
"It's too late to start something new."
"Stick to what you know."
"Let the younger ones build the future."

But here I was, 60 years old, designing my first mobile app.

People say youth is an advantage. And in some ways, it is. But experience? Experience will take you further than enthusiasm ever will. Experience gives you:

pattern recognition
intuition
resilience
patience
the ability to make decisions without ego
the ability to sense bullshit a mile away

I wasn't too old.
I was too seasoned to fail.

When you're young, you build with speed.
When you're older, you build with wisdom.

Glluz needed wisdom.

Of course, every big journey comes with shadows.
There were nights where I sat in front of my laptop, staring at figma
designs and feeling like I was reading a foreign language. Nights
where I wondered if I was being unrealistic. Nights where I
questioned whether people would understand the vision the way I
did.

Those moments are part of the process.
They test you.
They strip away ego.
They force you to choose between giving up and growing.

In those moments, I thought of my mother, my father's resilience,
my grandfather's quiet authority, and the structured English side of
my whānau (extended family). Each of them shaped the foundation
beneath my feet. The doubt didn't disappear, I just refused to let it
decide for me.

Here's the truth:
Starting Glluz forced me to re-learn myself.

All the titles I'd carried over the years, engineer, design, leader, none of them guaranteed success here. I had to become a student again. A beginner. An apprentice to a new world.

Being a beginner at 60 is humbling.
But it's also liberating.

It reminded me of something important:
You can reinvent yourself at any age.
You can start again at any age.
You can chase something new at any age.

People talk about legacy like it's something you leave behind once you're gone.
But sometimes legacy is built while you're still here changing lives in real time.

That's what Glluz started to feel like.

As the early stages of Glluz started to take shape, I found myself reflecting on why I was really doing this.
Connection.
Community.
Belonging.
Whānau (extended family).

These weren't just features for an app, they were cultural values.
They were Māori (Indigenous people of New Zealand) principles.
They were part of me.

In Māoridom (Māori worldview and culture), we don't see people as isolated individuals. We see them as part of a wider network ancestors behind us, whānau (extended family) beside us, generations ahead of us. Glluz wasn't just a sports app. It was a digital embodiment of that world view.

It was about creating communities.
It was about fostering relationships.
It was about reducing loneliness.
It was about bringing people together so they could be healthier in body, mind, and spirit.

It was about manaakitanga (care, hospitality, uplifting others).
It was about kotahitanga (unity).
It was about whanaungatanga (relationships and belonging).

It was, in many ways, a reflection of who I am.

And when your work reflects your identity, it becomes more than work.
It becomes a mission.

Glluz wasn't live yet. There was still a long road ahead, design, development, testing, branding, building teams, mistakes, setbacks, breakthroughs, everything that comes with creating something from scratch.

But this isn't about the technical build.
It's about the spark.
The calling.
The shift in identity.
The moment the next chapter of your life begins before you even realise it.

This was the beginning.

A Māori (Indigenous person of New Zealand) man in his 60s, shaped by rivers, mischief, music, family, culture, challenges, triumphs, and quiet determination, sitting at a laptop, sketching the blueprint for something the world hadn't seen yet.

For most of my life, my speech felt like a quiet negotiation between my mind and my mouth. Some days the words flowed effortlessly. Other days a single syllable could feel like a stone in my throat. But over time, something shifted. My speech became more fluid, the hiccups fewer, the pauses shorter. I began to understand the patterns of the words that tripped me up, the sounds that forced my tongue to stall, and instead of avoiding them, I chose to outgrow them.

I made it a mission to expand my vocabulary, not to sound clever, but to give myself more pathways to express my thoughts when one road felt blocked. I started learning new words, swapping out the ones that triggered hesitation for ones that flowed freely. Little by little, those substitutions became strengths. They weren't shortcuts, they were stepping stones. Each new word became a small victory, another tool that helped me stand taller in my conversations, my meetings, my storytelling.

As the blocks faded, my confidence grew. I could feel my voice taking shape, not just as sound but as presence. My ideas came out with clarity instead of caution. My passion wasn't hiding behind pauses anymore; it stood in front of me, proud and unfiltered. I began speaking without overthinking, without rehearsing each sentence in my head before letting it out. That freedom changed everything.

What once felt like a barrier became a bridge. The more I embraced my voice, the more I realised it had always been there, waiting for me to trust it. Now, when I speak, I do it with purpose. I do it with belief. My voice carries the weight of my ideas, my journey, and my plan, and I no longer hesitate to let it be heard.

And as I looked at that idea on the screen, glowing in the dim light of my living room, I felt something powerful.
Not fear.
Not uncertainty.
Not pressure.
But excitement.

The same excitement a boy feels when he first hops into the river, not knowing how deep the water is, but trusting that he'll learn by moving.

Glluz wasn't just an app.
It was my next river.
My next current.
My next test.
My next calling.

And I was ready to jump in.

CHAPTER 4

Part 2: Building the Whanau Behind the Vision

If Part 1 was the moment the spark caught fire, Part 2 became the slow and deliberate process of shaping that fire into something real. Ideas are beautiful things, but without action they are nothing more than passing thoughts. Glluz needed structure. It needed a heartbeat. It needed people who believed in the mission as much as I did. And that is when the concept of the Ambassador Program and the Community Hub started to take form.

From the beginning, I wanted Glluz to be more than a matchmaking tool for sports. I wanted it to be a living ecosystem of people who loved movement, competition, bonding and community. The Ambassador Program became the bridge between that vision and the real world. We created a system that allowed individuals to grow their own personal brand or business while growing ours. There is something powerful about giving people tools that help them build themselves. When you lift others, you rise together.

The Sports Community Hub became the soul of the platform. A place where people could share content, express their passion, and stay connected to a world that speaks their language. Sport is universal. You can walk into any country and mention a team, a player or a moment and immediately someone smiles in recognition. I wanted that global energy condensed into one digital space where people felt welcome, valued and seen. If Part 1 was about the idea, this part of the story was about giving that idea a home.

One thing I learned during this stage of the journey is that it is never too late to start something new. There is no expiry date on dreams. Age does not limit you. It arms you with experience, lessons and instincts that younger entrepreneurs simply do not have yet. I had spent decades solving complex problems, navigating corporate storms and working in high pressure environments. So when things got difficult, I did not crumble. I recalibrated.

Backing yourself is a non negotiable part of building anything meaningfully large. You need to trust your thinking and your ability to learn quickly. I spent countless hours researching. I joined online forums to understand user behaviour, studied how other sports communities grew, attended events and seminars, watched interviews with founders and tech leaders, and even signed up for competitor platforms as a user so I could study their strengths and weaknesses from the inside. I was a student again. Curious. Engaged. Determined to learn everything I possibly could.

But no matter how much you research, one truth will always remain. Your team matters. The people you build with can lift your vision or pull it apart. I was lucky to find the right developer early. He happened to be a passionate cricketer, and that shared love of sport helped him understand the emotional side of the project, not just the technical one. We spent hours drawing out user flows, redesigning screens, rethinking features and working through every tiny detail. His creativity sparked new ideas and my experience refined the direction. It was a partnership built on respect, honesty and a shared excitement for what we were building.

This stage of the journey required time, energy and relentless attention to detail. I quickly realised that building an app is not a one and done moment. It is a constant process of refining, correcting, testing and improving. I tested every feature as if I were the user. I asked questions. I pushed for clarity. I went through documents line by line. I forced myself to understand what I did not know yet. Crossing the Ts and dotting the Is is not a cliché. It is survival. If you invest in the details early, you save yourself years of pain later.

Once the app architecture took shape, I entered the next battlefield. Marketing. And let me tell you now, nothing prepares you for marketing better than being thrown into the deep end with no life jacket.

People say, If you build it, they will come. Well… they didn't. Not immediately. Not even close. When we first launched Glluz, I realised how little I knew about the world of digital marketing. I understood engineering, operations, leadership and tech. Marketing felt like an entirely different universe.

I had a bit of social media knowledge but nowhere near enough to confidently pour money into advertising. And when every pound I spent came straight from my savings, it felt like playing poker with real stakes. So I did what most founders in my position do. I made use of what was free.

I created brand new social media accounts under the Glluz name and decided to put my creativity to work. I used editing software to create small promotional videos, highlighted features, and experimented with different styles of content. I was proud of that first video. It felt like a moment. Like the start of something big. I hit publish and waited for the engagement to roll in. Nothing happened. I refreshed the page. Nothing. An hour later. Still nothing.

That silence could have knocked the wind out of me, but instead it lit a fire. I reminded myself why I had started this journey. So I created more. I played around with new ideas, different formats, and varied approaches. I purchased licensed sports clips from a content provider and layered them with AI generated voiceovers. I learned how to pace short videos for social media engagement. I learned how to use scheduling tools and set consistent posting patterns across all major platforms.

And slowly, very slowly, traction began to grow. A like here. A comment there. New followers. A small community started to form around the brand. I was excited, but still something was missing.

There was engagement, but not enough drive to convert those eyes into actual downloads.

So I decided to take a risk. I ran my first set of paid ads. I made mistakes. I wasted money. I misjudged my target audience. I learned hard lessons about click through rates, cost per install and the difference between vanity metrics and genuine conversions. But I kept adjusting. Kept experimenting. Kept pushing.

Eventually, the Glluz socials grew to over 25k followers and likes across platforms. It felt like validation. Proof that the brand had a voice and that people were listening. But here comes the twist that every new founder should understand.

Even with thousands of followers, the number of people actually downloading the app and converting was still low.

It hit me like a quiet punch. Being seen is not the same as being used. Attention is not the same as adoption. The journey I thought would be linear completely exposed itself as a maze filled with unexpected turns.

But this is where the story becomes valuable. Because the lack of downloads did not discourage me. It educated me. It taught me that growth requires far more than visibility. It requires strategy, psychology, design, trust and community activation. It requires a product that solves a real problem and marketing that speaks directly to the hearts of the people you want to serve.

Glluz was still becoming. And so was I. What mattered most was that I kept learning, kept adapting and kept evolving.

Because when you build something that comes from purpose, you do not stop at the first hurdle. Or the fifth. Or the fiftieth. You keep going.

It was around this time that I met a digital marketing consultant, one of the first people who truly understood the vision behind Glluz and where I was trying to take it. I brought them on board, and that decision shifted the entire trajectory of the project. Their insight cut through the noise and helped build the structure I didn't have at the start.

Together, we shaped a strategy that was simple, practical, and finally gave the app a real pathway forward:
Step 1: Drive installs.
Step 2: Convert free users into paying subscribers.

It's still early days, but the momentum is real, installs are coming in consistently, conversions are beginning to take shape, and for the first time, I can see the next phase clearly: scaling, expanding, and taking Glluz from an idea to a fully-fledged movement.

Wanting to give back and reconnect with people who shared the same fire I did, I organised a community event at our local art gallery, a night designed for entrepreneurs and small business owners to meet, talk, and support one another. I called it "speed pitching," a twist on speed dating, and it turned into an evening filled with energy, honesty, laughter, and the kind of unexpected connections that remind you why community matters.

Even at 60, that hunger hasn't faded, the drive to grow, to push boundaries, and to test myself mentally just as fiercely as I once did on the sports field. I've built my startup from the ground up, fully self-funded, powered only by vision, strategy, and the stubborn belief that I could turn Glluz into a million-pound company, not just for profit, but for purpose.

That same competitive streak has followed me through every stage of my life, sometimes in serious arenas and sometimes in ways that make me laugh when I look back on them. I once became a four-time oyster-eating champion, a title that still raises eyebrows whenever it comes up in conversation. The year ITV turned up to film the event, I finished second. That didn't sit well with me. It wasn't about the oysters or the trophy. It was the idea of not finishing what I had started, of letting something slip without answering it.

So the following year, after attending a friend's wedding in Wales, I didn't head home to rest like a sensible person might. Instead, I got in the car and drove all the way to Whitstable in the southeast of England. Tired, and running on stubborn determination, I entered again and reclaimed the title that very same day. It wasn't glamorous, but it was familiar. That refusal to leave something unresolved. That need to prove to myself, more than anyone else, that I could still rise to the challenge.

That mindset has always felt older than my body and younger than my years. In my head, I still feel like that determined twenty-five-year-old rugby player, the one who believed effort could outlast fatigue and grit could outwork doubt. The one who saw competition not as opposition, but as a mirror. A way to measure who you are when things get uncomfortable.

But bodies tell the truth eventually, even when the mind refuses to listen.

Hanging up my rugby boots at fifty-seven wasn't a moment of defeat. It was a moment of honesty. Rugby had shaped me. It had given me discipline, brotherhood, resilience, and a place to burn off everything I didn't yet know how to say out loud. The boots carried years of mud, bruises, laughter, injuries, and quiet pride. They were never just equipment. They were a symbol of who I had been and how I had lived.

Letting them go wasn't about losing competitiveness. That never left. It was about recognising that the fight had changed shape. The field was different now. The challenges were no longer measured in tackles and metres gained, but in endurance of a different kind. Mental strength. Emotional resilience. Purpose. Legacy.

When I hung up those boots, I wasn't stepping away from competition. I was stepping into a new one. One that asked me to channel the same hunger, the same refusal to settle, the same drive to improve, into building, creating, and leading in new ways. My body may not keep pace the way it once did, but the engine inside me hasn't slowed. It's just learned where to run next.

CHAPTER 4

Part 3: A Founders Second Wind

There comes a moment in every journey when the road you have travelled quietly intersects with the road you are about to build. Not with a dramatic announcement or a perfectly timed sign, but with a persistent nudge that refuses to be ignored. For me, that moment arrived without ceremony. No fanfare. No lightning bolt. Just an idea that kept tapping me on the shoulder, politely at first, then with increasing insistence, until I finally accepted that it wasn't going anywhere.

Glluz began as a feeling long before it became a product. A spark, then a pull. I had lived the pain point myself. Wanting to play. Wanting to connect. Wanting to turn up without feeling like the odd one out. I had also watched countless others stand on the sidelines, not because they lacked ability, but because confidence is not something everyone can summon on demand. It's easy to forget that when confidence comes naturally to you. It's invisible until it isn't. That realisation sat with me for a long time.

But turning a feeling into a functioning app required a version of me that didn't yet exist. It demanded skills I hadn't used before, decisions I hadn't faced, and a willingness to step into uncertainty without the comfort of experience to lean on.

At sixty, I realised I wasn't just launching an app. I was launching myself into an entirely new world. Entrepreneurship doesn't care how many decades you've spent mastering other disciplines. It doesn't bow to past success. It asks different questions. It demands a different kind of wiring. Not technical frameworks or architectural diagrams, but mental agility. The kind that forces you to grow, adapt, unlearn, and occasionally sit there wondering how you managed to break something that worked perfectly five minutes earlier.

I had always been competitive, driven, and resilient, but diving into a startup that was self funded, self built, and powered purely by belief pushed me into deeper water than anything before it. There was no safety net. No corporate buffer. No one to escalate to. Just conviction, effort, and a growing collection of browser tabs that multiplied faster than I could close them.

I carried my background with me, the values that had shaped how I approached challenge, responsibility, and pressure. They taught me to stand firm, to push forward, and to trust myself even when external validation was slow to arrive. That mindset turned out to be essential, because the startup world rewards momentum long before it rewards certainty.

In the early days, I found myself sitting at the kitchen table staring at a blank page. No analysts. No investors. No advisory board. Just me, a cup of tea, and the uncomfortable truth that a good idea without a plan is just a hobby. I didn't need inspiration. I needed structure.

So I wrote everything down. What Glluz was. Who it was for. The problems it solved. How we would grow. How we would keep people coming back. How we would eventually make money without losing the soul of what we were building. It was rough, messy, and constantly changing, but it gave me something to work with. That blank page slowly stopped feeling intimidating and started feeling useful.

It became my compass.
And eventually, my map.

What I hadn't anticipated was how deeply I would need to reinvent myself to understand an entirely new discipline. Overnight, my thinking shifted. I wasn't approaching problems like a telecom architect anymore. I was thinking like a digital founder. Less about perfection. More about progress. Less about final designs. More about iteration.

I immersed myself in product market fit, marketing funnels, customer behaviour, pricing psychology, user journeys, retention metrics, and sales dynamics. Some nights it felt like learning a new language with no subtitles. Other nights, everything suddenly made sense and I wondered why I hadn't done this sooner. Every mistake became data. Every misstep became feedback. Pride had no place here. Curiosity did.

Once the development team brought the app to life, I ran headfirst into the next reality check. Building it was only half the job. People actually needed to find it.

So I built a strategy from the ground up.

First came awareness. Telling the story through social media, community videos, LinkedIn posts, organic content, and real conversations that didn't feel like sales pitches.

Then acquisition. Driving installs through targeted campaigns, search optimisation, App Store positioning, and messaging that spoke to confidence, connection, and ease rather than pressure.

Then activation. Making sure users felt value immediately. That the app felt intuitive, welcoming, and safe. A place where connection felt natural, not awkward.

Then retention. Keeping people engaged through updates, features, notifications, and a genuine community-first mindset.

Finally, monetisation. Clear pricing. Fair value. Upgrades that felt optional, not manipulative.

This wasn't just strategy.
It was craft.
It was storytelling with intent.

To grow sustainably, Glluz needed a proper revenue engine. I studied competitors, analysed patterns, built subscription tiers, tested approaches, and refined onboarding so users understood the value without needing a manual. I created a free plan and a premium plan. Added features that genuinely mattered. Introduced upgrades thoughtfully.

Then I took it one step further.

I logged into the Apple App Store and Google Play Console and created my first promotional codes. Technical, fiddly, mildly infuriating at times, but strangely satisfying once they worked.

One decision mattered more than most.

The first thousand users would receive a free upgrade to Glluz Premium.

Not just a promotion, but an invitation. A way to say, if you're here early, you matter. If you help shape this, you're part of it. A signal that this wasn't just another app chasing numbers.

People responded. Codes were redeemed. Early momentum built. A real community began forming, one user at a time.

If Glluz was going to scale, it needed real support. Not a hidden email address buried in a menu, but help people could actually use. So I built FAQs, chat support, troubleshooting flows, user guides, community guidelines, and feedback loops. The work no one applauds, but everyone relies on.

I learned quickly that selling Glluz was never about features.

People don't buy apps.
They buy belonging.

They buy confidence.
They buy relief from problems they rarely say out loud.

Glluz became a story I could tell. For the shy person wanting to join a game. For the newcomer to a club. For someone new to a city. For anyone craving connection but unsure where to start.

The story became the product.
The product became the mission.
The mission became the movement.

There's a belief that startups are a young person's game, fuelled by caffeine and chaos. But age doesn't dull hunger. It sharpens it. It strips away nonsense. It replaces speed with clarity.

At sixty, I brought experience, discipline, resilience, and a healthy intolerance for wasted time. My body might not move like it did on the rugby field, but my mind is still sharp, competitive, and hungry.

Organising a community speed-pitching night at the local art gallery felt like closing a loop. A room full of founders, small business owners, and creators sharing ideas, challenges, and ambition. It reminded me exactly why I started building Glluz in the first place. To help people find their place. Their people.

That's who I am.
A mix of discipline, lived experience, and determination.
Forged through failure, persistence, and a refusal to stand still.

Glluz is still growing. Promo codes are live. Installs are rising. Conversions are building. The community is forming piece by piece.

What I know now is this. Building an app isn't just a business journey. It's a personal one.

I'm not just building technology. I'm building something that reflects who I am, what I've lived through, and my refusal to stop evolving.

And the story doesn't end here.

In the next chapter, I step further behind the scenes, into the late nights, unexpected costs, moments of doubt, and breakthroughs that shaped what came next.

This is the journey of Glluz.
This is the journey of resilience.
This is the journey of a founder who refuses to slow down.

CHAPTER 5

Part 1: When Speed Replaced Certainty

The next chapter of my story did not begin with a dramatic decision
or a bold announcement. It began with a feeling that crept in quietly
and refused to leave. A sense that the ground beneath technology was
no longer stable in the way I had known for most of my career.
Change was no longer incremental. It was no longer predictable. It
was accelerating in a way that felt both exhilarating and unsettling.

Artificial intelligence had crossed a threshold.

Not in theory. Not in research papers. In practice.

It was no longer confined to chatbots answering questions or
automations handling simple workflows. It was reasoning. Planning.
Adapting. Learning across time. Making decisions with increasing
autonomy. Systems were no longer waiting for instructions. They
were beginning to anticipate needs.

And once that happened, everything changed.

At first, the shift announced itself through conversations rather than
code. Clients stopped asking exploratory questions. The curiosity
phase ended almost overnight. No one wanted to talk about whether
AI was relevant anymore. That question disappeared as if it had
never existed. In its place came urgency.

How quickly can we deploy this
How deeply can it integrate
How far can it go
What happens if we do not move now

The tone had changed. The pressure was real.

Founders wanted answers immediately. Not conceptual explanations. Not future possibilities. They wanted outcomes. Teams wanted support that did not slow down or sleep. Leaders wanted intelligence that could see around corners rather than react after damage had already been done.

AI was no longer a tool to experiment with. It was becoming an operational expectation.

That reality forced me into a period of reflection I had not anticipated.

I had spent decades working in environments where reliability mattered more than novelty. Where systems were designed to last. Where change followed governance, process, and testing. Telecommunications had taught me to value stability, precision, and responsibility. Networks carried real consequences. When things failed, people felt it immediately.

This new landscape operated differently.

AI did not wait for permission. It evolved whether organisations were ready or not. Models improved at a pace that outstripped documentation. Best practices expired faster than they could be agreed upon. Something that felt cutting edge one month felt dated the next.

I realised quickly that mastery had a shelf life.

That was not easy to accept.

There is comfort in expertise. In knowing that your experience gives you authority. In recognising patterns because you have seen them before. Suddenly, the patterns were mutating too fast to rely on memory alone. Yesterday's solutions were becoming constraints.

I had to decide who I was going to be in this phase of my life.

I could resist the pace and anchor myself to familiar frameworks. Or I could accept that certainty was no longer the currency of leadership. Adaptability was.

That decision marked the true turning point.

I stopped thinking about building products.

Products assume completion. They imply stability. AI did not behave that way. What made sense instead was capability. Something modular. Something adaptive. Something designed to evolve alongside the organisations using it.

Glluztech needed to become an ecosystem.

That shift was not theoretical. It changed how I approached everything. Instead of asking what features we should build, I asked what people were actually struggling with. And what I heard repeatedly was not a lack of tools. It was overload.

Businesses were drowning in dashboards. Data flowed faster than interpretation. Automation piled on automation. Complexity increased under the banner of efficiency. People did not need more technology. They needed coherence.

They needed intelligence that simplified rather than complicated.

That insight became foundational.

AI needed to feel like a teammate, not an interface. Something that understood context, intention, culture, and priorities. Something that could operate within a business rather than sitting on top of it.

As I looked outward, the scale of transformation across industries became impossible to ignore.

Healthcare was shifting toward predictive diagnostics, using machine learning to identify risk before symptoms surfaced. Education explored adaptive tutors capable of adjusting to each student in real time. Retail embraced generative systems that could build campaigns, strategies, and content in minutes rather than weeks. Financial services leaned into autonomous compliance and real time risk analysis that once required entire teams.

Telecommunications, my original home, began to transform into something barely recognisable.

Networks started predicting outages before they occurred. Voice systems evolved into reasoning agents capable of understanding intent, sentiment, and context. Infrastructure stopped being passive. It became intelligent.

AI was no longer an enhancement. It was becoming the backbone.

Seeing that made my role clear.

Glluztech needed to sit precisely where innovation met practicality. Where vision translated into execution. Where ambition was grounded by responsibility.

But stepping into that space required risk.

It meant leaving behind proven frameworks. It meant entering environments where compliance standards were still forming and ethical boundaries were being debated in real time. Every investor conversation carried greater weight. Every partnership required not just technical competence but moral clarity.

Power without direction becomes noise.

So I immersed myself fully.

I studied agentic systems capable of independent operation. Memory architectures that allowed AI to retain long term understanding. Reasoning layers that enabled planning rather than reaction. Retrieval systems that grounded intelligence in real data rather than hallucination.

I explored how autonomy emerged and how it could be constrained responsibly. How trust could be built. How humans and AI could collaborate without either being diminished.

At the same time, I had to evolve emotionally.

There were moments when the pace felt overwhelming. When the velocity of change triggered doubt. Questions surfaced quietly but persistently.

Could I keep up
Could I lead in an industry that refused to slow down
Could I build something meaningful while the rules were still being written

Those moments were real. They were not dramatic. They were internal. They arrived late at night after long days of learning, testing, discarding, and rebuilding.

But with each breakthrough, the vision sharpened.

People did not need more complexity. They needed clarity. They needed intelligence that communicated naturally. Systems that understood human intention rather than forcing humans to adapt to machines.

That insight reshaped everything.

Glluztech stopped being about automation. It became about capability. AI that could organise entire workflows. Agents that understood goals, culture, and communication style. Systems that operated alongside people rather than replacing them.

This was not about replacing humans. It was about amplifying them.

And that was only the beginning.

CHAPTER 5

Part 2: Building While Everything Was Still Moving

By the time the shape of Glluztech began to feel real in my hands, I had already come to terms with something that quietly unsettles a lot of people in technology. There would be no finish line. No moment where I could stop, look around, and say I had finally caught up. The industry was not racing toward a stable destination. It was accelerating away from certainty altogether.

That understanding did not arrive in a dramatic flash. It settled slowly, through observation, frustration, and a growing sense that every time I thought I had a grip on the landscape, it rearranged itself underneath me. Models improved overnight. Tools evolved weekly. Entire approaches became outdated before they had fully matured. At first, that pace felt intimidating. Eventually, it became clarifying.

If nothing was going to stand still, then neither could I.

That realisation changed how I worked in practical ways. I stopped chasing perfection, because perfection assumed a final form that no longer existed. I stopped trying to predict what things would look like years ahead, because prediction in a moving environment is often just disguised nostalgia. Instead, I focused on building things that could survive change. Systems that could flex without snapping. Architectures that could accept new ideas without collapsing under their own weight.

That required a different kind of discipline than traditional product building.

It required humility.

I had to become comfortable discarding ideas I genuinely liked. Not because they were bad, but because something better had emerged. I had to accept that months of effort could be made irrelevant by a single breakthrough somewhere else in the world. That stung at times, especially when pride wanted to get involved. But I learned quickly that clinging to outdated thinking was far more dangerous than letting go of good work.

Relevance had a cost. This was it.

The first real test of that mindset came through conversations with clients. Not the polished sales calls or the enthusiastic early adopters, but the honest, sometimes tired discussions that happened once people trusted me enough to drop the performance.

A pattern began to repeat itself across industries.

People were not asking for artificial intelligence as an abstract concept. They were not excited by buzzwords or impressed by demonstrations alone. What they were asking for was relief.

Relief from decision fatigue. Relief from constant operational friction. Relief from the feeling that no matter how hard they worked, there was always more to do than time allowed. Founders spoke about running companies that had grown faster than their internal structures could support. Enterprise teams described being buried under systems that no longer talked to each other. Leaders carried the weight of responsibility but lacked the mental space to think clearly about what came next.

What united them was not ambition.

It was exhaustion.

They did not want another platform to learn. Another dashboard to check. Another tool that promised efficiency but demanded attention. They wanted something that could think alongside them. Something that could filter noise, highlight what mattered, and support momentum without needing constant supervision.

That insight reshaped everything.

We stopped designing agents as tools and started designing them as participants. An agent that answered questions was useful. An agent that understood why a question was being asked was something else entirely. Context mattered more than capability. Memory mattered more than speed.

This was where the idea of intelligent teams truly took form in my mind.

I began to imagine a future where individuals had access to capabilities that once required entire departments. Strategy, analysis, planning, communication, execution. Not delivered through layers of software interfaces, but through conversation. Systems that learned over time. That adapted to tone. That recognised patterns in behaviour and adjusted accordingly.

In that future, small businesses could scale with the confidence of enterprises. Large organisations could regain agility without chaos. People could spend more time thinking, creating, and leading, and less time managing administrative drag.

It was an ambitious vision, and turning it into reality meant going far deeper than surface level innovation.

I immersed myself in the foundations.

How memory could persist without becoming brittle. How reasoning could remain grounded without drifting into unpredictability. How autonomy could be constrained without suffocating intelligence. How systems could explain themselves rather than simply produce outputs.

These were not theoretical exercises. Every choice had consequences. Every shortcut introduced risk. Every optimisation traded one benefit for another. Trust was being built quietly, decision by decision, line by line.

There were long stretches where progress felt invisible.s.

Weeks spent refining logic flows that no user would ever see. Weeks where models behaved in ways that forced us back to first principles. Weeks where the market shifted faster than we could respond, making us question whether we were solving the right problems at the right time.

Those periods tested my patience more than any visible failure ever could.

But they also taught me something essential. Urgency alone does not create innovation. Alignment does. Moving fast in the wrong direction only increases the distance from what matters. Learning when to pause, reassess, and recalibrate became just as important as maintaining momentum.

Failure became a teacher rather than a verdict.

Sometimes the architecture was too rigid. Sometimes the data was misaligned. Sometimes the timing was simply wrong. Each setback revealed something new, not just about the technology, but about how I responded under pressure.

I learned that building in an emerging space demands emotional regulation as much as technical skill. Panic leads to rushed decisions. Ego blocks learning. Fear slows progress. Confidence must exist without arrogance. Curiosity has to override defensiveness.

And perhaps most importantly, I learned that no one builds the future alone.

As Glluztech evolved, collaboration became the true engine of growth. Conversations with other founders sparked ideas that would never have surfaced in isolation. Advisors offered perspective shaped by experience rather than speculation. Developers challenged assumptions through implementation rather than theory.

Late night discussions in digital communities often unlocked insights that saved weeks of work. A single conversation could shift an entire roadmap. I stopped thinking in terms of competition and started thinking in terms of contribution. The ecosystem was too vast and too complex for territorial thinking. Those who shared knowledge accelerated together.

Leadership in this space, I discovered, was not about having answers.

It was about asking better questions.

As the systems matured, my sense of responsibility deepened alongside them. AI does not exist in a vacuum. It shapes decisions. It influences behaviour. It amplifies outcomes. Without intention, it can reinforce bias, accelerate harm, or create unhealthy dependency.

Building responsibly was not optional.

It meant embedding guardrails. Designing transparency. Prioritising explainability. Ensuring autonomy always operated within defined boundaries. It also meant recognising when not to build something.

There were ideas that looked powerful but felt wrong. Opportunities that prioritised efficiency at the expense of humanity. Walking away from those was not easy, especially in an environment that rewards speed and novelty. But integrity mattered more than momentum.

As the vision sharpened, so did the sense of purpose.

Glluztech was no longer simply responding to demand. It was shaping how people experienced intelligence. It was redefining what support looked like in a digital world. It was creating space for humans to think clearly in an environment that often feels overwhelming.

The journey was still unstable. Each breakthrough introduced new challenges. Each advancement raised new questions. The industry continued to evolve faster than regulation, culture, and understanding.

But something fundamental had shifted inside me.

I was no longer trying to keep up.

I was moving with it.

And that made all the difference.

CHAPTER 5

Part 3: When Vision Met Scale and the stakes Became Real

There is a moment in every journey when progress stops feeling like exploration and starts feeling like responsibility. Up until then, everything carries a sense of permission. You are allowed to try things. Allowed to break things. Allowed to learn out loud. Mistakes are framed as lessons, and curiosity is rewarded more than certainty.

Then something shifts.

You realise people are no longer just watching what you are doing. They are depending on it.

That was the moment Glluztech crossed into its next phase.

What we were building had moved beyond whiteboards, prototypes, and conversations that ended with "imagine if." The systems were live. They were embedded. They were influencing decisions that shaped real outcomes. Businesses were no longer using our work as a test. They were trusting it as part of how they operated.

That changes the temperature of everything.

At small scale, failure is forgiving. At larger scale, failure echoes. It touches teams you have never met. It affects timelines you are not sitting inside. It erodes confidence far faster than it builds. The margin for error tightens quietly but decisively, and the weight of that reality settles on your shoulders whether you invite it or not.

I felt it almost immediately.

Design decisions stopped being abstract. Architecture choices were no longer about elegance alone. They became about resilience. About behaviour under stress. About what happened not when things worked, but when they didn't. Because at scale, something always breaks eventually.

That was when I truly understood the difference between building technology and leading a technology company.

The questions in my head changed.

They were no longer only about how fast something could run or how clever a system appeared. They became questions about trust. About longevity. About whether intelligence could grow without losing coherence. Whether capability could scale without turning brittle. Whether speed could coexist with care.

It would have been comforting to slow everything down. To pull back and regain a sense of control.

But the world was not slowing with me.

AI adoption was accelerating across every sector. Companies that had once been sceptical were now scrambling. Leaders who had dismissed the technology were suddenly asking how quickly it could be implemented. Regulators were watching closely. Investors were sharpening their expectations. Partners were no longer impressed by novelty. They wanted reliability.

The pressure was subtle but relentless.

This forced a deeper evolution inside Glluztech.

We stopped thinking in terms of impressive features and started thinking in terms of dependable capability. The goal shifted from making something look intelligent to making it behave intelligently in real conditions. Success was no longer about standing out. It was about fitting in so seamlessly that the technology disappeared into the background of daily work.

The best compliment became silence.

If the system was doing its job, people didn't talk about it. They just relied on it.

To get there, we had to become obsessed with context.

An intelligent system that lacks context is just fast confusion. Agents could not simply execute instructions. They needed to understand the environment they were operating in. The industry. The constraints. The culture. The tone. The risk tolerance of the organisation using them.

A system supporting healthcare could not behave like one supporting a creative agency. A tool assisting a regulated enterprise could not operate with the same freedom as one helping a founder brainstorm ideas late at night. Intelligence had to be situational, not generic.

Memory became central to that shift.

Not memory in the shallow sense of storing facts, but memory as continuity. Remembering preferences. Recognising patterns. Understanding intent across time. Learning how a business behaved when under pressure versus when confident. Noticing when priorities subtly changed long before anyone announced them.

This was where the idea of long horizon intelligence truly took shape for me.

Most systems respond moment by moment. Very few can reason across time. I wanted agents that understood the arc of a business, not just the task in front of them. Systems that could sense momentum, anticipate friction, and adapt as organisations evolved.

Achieving that required restraint.

It meant resisting the temptation to automate everything simply because we could. It meant accepting that autonomy without guardrails was not innovation. It was risk disguised as progress. We focused instead on orchestration. Human involvement where judgement mattered. Autonomy where it added genuine value. Structure everywhere.

That balance was never fixed. It shifted constantly depending on industry, maturity, and use case. Designing for that flexibility became one of the hardest and most important challenges we faced.

And then there were the people.

Growth does not just multiply systems. It multiplies relationships. Teams expand. Collaborators increase. Expectations diverge. Alignment becomes something you work at daily rather than assume.

Leadership in that environment demanded clarity.

I learned quickly that vision cannot be delivered once and left alone. It has to be reinforced constantly. Through decisions. Through priorities. Through what you build and, just as importantly, what you choose not to build.

People need to know why the work matters, not just what the work is.

Without that shared understanding, speed turns into chaos.

At the same time, leadership required honesty. I did not have all the answers. No one did. Pretending otherwise would have been reckless.

So I leaned into transparency. I spoke openly about uncertainty. I invited disagreement. Some of the most valuable insights came from unexpected places. From engineers challenging assumptions. From partners highlighting blind spots. From clients articulating frustrations we had not fully seen.

Listening became a strategic advantage.

Still, doubt did not disappear.

It showed up late at night, when momentum slowed and the noise faded. Questions surfaced that daylight often drowned out. Were we building the right things. Were we moving too fast. Or not fast enough. Were we protecting what mattered. Were we ready for what was coming next.

I learned that confidence is not the absence of those questions. It is the ability to keep moving while carrying them.

As Glluztech grew, scrutiny increased. Early adopters were replaced by cautious decision makers. Proof mattered more than promise. Metrics replaced enthusiasm. Reliability replaced excitement.

We welcomed that shift.

It forced discipline. It forced maturity. It forced us to earn trust repeatedly rather than assume it.

This was also when the broader implications of our work became impossible to ignore. AI was reshaping how work was done. How decisions were made. How power moved within organisations. The systems we built influenced culture as much as efficiency.

That demanded values.

Not as marketing language, but as operating principles. Transparency. Explainability. Human agency. Augmentation rather than replacement. Not because they sounded good, but because they were essential.

Technology without values drifts. And drifting power is dangerous. Through all of this, one truth became clear. The future was not about building smarter machines.

It was about building better relationships between humans and intelligence.

Systems that clarified rather than confused. That supported rather than overwhelmed. That extended human capability instead of erasing it.

Glluztech was becoming a bridge.

Between complexity and clarity. Between ambition and execution. Between what was possible and what was practical. And the bridge was holding. But bridges exist for a reason. They lead somewhere.

And on the other side of this phase, something larger was already taking shape.

CHAPTER 5

Part 4: Finding the right Companions for the
Road Ahead

There comes a point in any long journey where effort alone stops
being the deciding factor. You can work harder, stay up later, drink
more coffee, push more code, chase more ideas, but eventually
progress demands something else. It demands choice. Not just what
you are building, but how you are building it, and more importantly,
who or what you are building alongside.

For me, that realisation did not arrive with a dramatic announcement
or a perfectly timed breakthrough. It arrived quietly, late at night,
long after sensible people had gone to bed. The house was silent. The
screen in front of me glowed far too brightly for the hour. I was
testing yet another AI model, watching it respond, watching how it
reasoned, how it hesitated, how it filled gaps when information was
missing, and how it behaved when it was unsure.

By that stage, I had stopped being impressed by clever answers
alone. I had seen too many of them. What I was paying attention to
was how the system behaved when things were unclear. Whether it
rushed. Whether it asked questions. Whether it admitted uncertainty.
Whether it tried to bluff its way through or quietly worked its way
around the problem like someone who actually understood the
weight of getting it wrong.

The world of AI had become noisy by then. Every week brought a
new model release, a new benchmark, a new claim of superiority.
Faster. Bigger. Cheaper. Smarter. Social feeds were filled with
charts, leaderboards, hot takes, and breathless predictions about who
was winning and who was finished. If you listened too closely, you
could lose weeks just keeping up with the noise.

But when you are building something real, something meant to sit inside businesses and affect real people's work and decisions, that noise fades quickly. You stop asking which model scores highest on a test and start asking whether you trust it to sit beside someone making a serious decision on a tired Tuesday afternoon.

I began to notice that different systems felt different to work with. Not technically, but emotionally. Some were brilliant at speed, firing back answers instantly, confident to the point of arrogance. They were impressive, no doubt, but they sometimes felt brittle, like a clever student who panics the moment the question changes slightly. Others moved more slowly, but with a kind of deliberate care. They asked for clarification. They paused. They reasoned. They felt less like machines trying to impress and more like thoughtful collaborators trying to help.

That distinction mattered to me more than I expected.

I found myself gravitating toward tools that valued alignment and reasoning over raw bravado. Systems that did not pretend to know everything. Systems that were comfortable saying, "Let's think this through." Tools that behaved less like engines and more like colleagues you would actually want to sit next to in a meeting.

At the same time, I could not ignore the sheer capability of platforms built for scale. Some ecosystems offered infrastructure strength that was hard to beat. They handled massive workloads, multimodal inputs, complex integrations, and enterprise environments with a level of reliability that made them invaluable. Others pushed the frontier of general intelligence, showing a breadth of capability that still occasionally made me lean back in my chair and laugh, not because it was funny, but because it was absurdly impressive.

I stopped thinking of these tools as competitors.

I started thinking of them as personalities.

One felt cautious and reflective, like the colleague who reads the room before speaking. Another felt expansive and creative, full of ideas and connections you had not considered. Another felt practical and grounded, brilliant at getting things done at scale without fuss. Each had strengths. Each had blind spots. None were perfect. And that was fine.

Choosing between them stopped being about loyalty or trends and became about fit.

Certain problems demanded depth and care. Others demanded speed and reach. Some needed strict reasoning and restraint. Others benefited from creative exploration. Once I accepted that no single system needed to do everything, the pressure lifted. I was no longer searching for the best AI. I was looking for the right one for the moment.

That shift changed everything about how Glluztech evolved.

Instead of locking ourselves into a single provider or architecture, we built for flexibility. For orchestration. For intelligence layered on top of intelligence. Tasks could be routed to the systems best suited to handle them. Outputs could be cross checked. Perspectives could be blended. Agents could collaborate in ways that mirrored how human teams actually work.

A compliance agent might rely on one kind of reasoning. A marketing agent might lean into another. A strategic planning agent might consult several voices before offering a conclusion. The real value was not in any one model, but in how they were choreographed together.

I remember watching one early agent navigate a complex business scenario involving staffing pressure, cash flow risk, and growth ambition. One model produced a fast, confident recommendation. Another slowed everything down, surfaced risks, and asked uncomfortable questions. A third reframed the entire problem, suggesting a path no one in the room had considered.

None of them were wrong.

But only one felt right for the human decision maker sitting across from the screen.

That was the moment it fully clicked.

AI is not just a tool you deploy. It is a presence you invite in.

And just like people, different presences suit different environments.

Some thrive in chaos. Some bring calm. Some push relentlessly forward. Others stabilise. Some challenge you. Some support you. The mistake is assuming one personality fits every situation.

As this understanding deepened, it began to shape how I spoke to founders and leaders as well. Instead of recommending platforms, I started asking different questions. How do you like to think. How do you make decisions. Do you want speed or certainty. Do you value exploration or precision. How much ambiguity are you comfortable living with.

Those answers mattered far more than any spec sheet.

AI adoption stopped being about features and started being about alignment.

And when alignment is right, everything feels easier.

That philosophy extended beyond technology into culture. We built systems that encouraged reflection instead of reaction. That surfaced trade offs rather than hiding them behind confidence. That invited human judgement instead of trying to replace it. The goal was never to remove people from the loop, but to give them better loops to work within.

What emerged was not automation for its own sake, but partnership.

Humans setting direction, values, and meaning. AI handling complexity, repetition, and scale. Each supporting the other, neither pretending to be the hero of the story.

There were still risks, of course. There always are. Models misbehaved. Experiments failed. Ideas that looked brilliant on paper collapsed under real world pressure. There were moments of frustration when something that should have worked simply did not. Moments when I questioned whether any of this would ever feel stable.

But there was also confidence.

Confidence that we were building with intention. Confidence that the systems we created would grow responsibly. Confidence that we were not chasing every shiny new release, but shaping something coherent in a world that often feels fragmented.

Looking back, this chapter was not really about choosing AI tools at all.

It was about discernment.

About learning when to move fast and when to pause. About resisting the urge to chase everything. About accepting that leadership in technology is not about knowing all the answers, but about asking better questions and listening carefully to what comes back.

Somewhere along the way, without a ceremony or announcement, I stopped being just a builder.

I became a steward.

Someone responsible not just for what was possible, but for what was appropriate. Not just for innovation, but for impact.

The road ahead was still uncertain. It always would be. But for the first time, I felt aligned with the companions I had chosen for the journey, human and artificial alike.

And that made the future feel less intimidating.

Even exciting. And it's continuing…

Reflection

When I look back across the chapters of my life now, I see a story shaped less by straight lines and more by tides. Movement forward, moments of stillness, times of being pulled under, and long stretches where progress was measured simply by the act of continuing. My journey has not been defined by perfection or certainty. It has been shaped by growth, loss, resilience, reinvention, and a deep connection to who I am and where I come from. In its rawness and honesty, I hope others recognise parts of themselves. Especially those who have struggled to find their voice, those who have had to start again later than planned, and those who have learned that life rarely offers a clear or predictable path.

My whakapapa (genealogy, lineage) sits at the heart of everything. Ngāti Porou (tribe from the East Coast of New Zealand) and Ngā Puhi (tribe from Northland, New Zealand) are not just names or affiliations. They are living influences that shaped how I stand, how I listen, and how I move through the world. My father came from the East Coast, raised in a large family where loyalty, responsibility, and community were not concepts but daily practice. My mother carried the strength of Ngā Puhi (tribe from Northland, New Zealand), stepping into Taranaki at a time when old tribal tensions still existed, and choosing patience, kindness, and integrity over resistance. Together, they taught me lessons no classroom ever could. They showed me mana (authority, prestige, spiritual power) not as dominance, but as steadiness. They showed me resilience not as hardness, but as consistency. They taught me that even when the ground shifts beneath you, you can remain anchored in who you are.

One of the defining chapters of my life arrived far earlier than I expected. Losing my father in my early twenties cracked something open inside me that I did not yet have the maturity to fully understand. At that age, you assume your parents are permanent fixtures. You believe your father will always be there with a nod, a quiet word, a presence that steadies the room. His passing left a silence that felt too large for language. He was a Māori (Indigenous person of New Zealand) Warden, a man respected deeply in our community. He carried authority without ego, leadership without noise, and service without expectation. People trusted him. Children felt safe around him. When trouble surfaced, he calmed it. At his tangi (funeral rites, mourning ceremony), I understood something that has stayed with me ever since. A person's true measure is not found in possessions or status, but in the impact they leave in the hearts of others. My father left mana (authority, prestige, spiritual power). He left example. He left a standard his children would spend a lifetime trying to honour.

Losing my mother later in life reopened grief in a different way. Her passing reminded me just how deeply our parents carve their values into us. She was a woman who earned belonging through grace and strength, who never demanded acceptance but lived in a way that made it inevitable. Her death taught me tenderness. It taught me patience. It reminded me that life is fragile, and that the people who raise us continue to guide us long after they are gone. Through memory, instinct, and spirit, they remain present. Their lessons become the compass we follow, often without realising it.

Grief forced me to reflect on my own relationships. On moments where communication could have been clearer. On times when pride stood in the way of vulnerability. On opportunities for connection that I might have handled differently. Those reflections humbled me. They taught me to value presence over being right, to appreciate those who stayed, and to understand that respect is something you live, not something you demand.

One of the greatest sources of pride in my life is my children. Watching them grow into grounded, capable, thoughtful adults has been one of my most meaningful achievements. They built careers, formed strong relationships, and moved through the world with confidence and emotional intelligence. They navigated challenges with maturity that continues to impress me. I see in them the hopes I once held quietly in my heart. I also honour their mother for the role she played in shaping them. She guided them with discipline, patience, and love. Parenting is not easy, and guiding children into adulthood requires consistency and sacrifice. She did that with grace, and the evidence lives in the people our children have become.

Then there are my grandchildren. Each time I see them, I am reminded that our stories do not end with us. In them, I see my parents' smiles, their spirit, and the continuation of our whakapapa (genealogy, lineage). They bring joy without condition. They remind me of curiosity, innocence, and renewal. They are living proof that legacy is not about what we leave behind, but what continues forward.

Though distance separates me from my brother and sister, our connection has never weakened. Oceans may stretch between us, but the bond built in childhood remains intact. We share the same memories, the same values, the same grounding. Every conversation reinforces the truth that whānau (extended family) is not measured by proximity, but by connection.

Growing up with a speech stammer shaped me more than I understood at the time. Some days words flowed freely. Other days they tangled and resisted. But I refused to let silence define me. I adapted. I expanded my language. I rebuilt confidence piece by piece. To anyone who struggles with their voice, I want you to know this. Your voice is not broken. It is becoming. And when you learn to work with it, it carries depth others cannot replicate.

Adulthood tested me in different ways. Career pressure. Financial strain. Relationship wounds. Periods where direction felt unclear. But each struggle sharpened something within me. Failure taught discipline. Heartbreak taught empathy. Doubt taught patience. My culture reminded me that my ancestors navigated vast oceans guided only by stars and instinct. That knowledge gave me faith that I could navigate my own life with the tools I had been given.

One of the greatest surprises of my later years was discovering that ambition does not expire. Stepping into technology, AI, and entrepreneurship at a stage when many slow down reignited something in me. Learning became energising again. Curiosity returned. I studied, attended events, joined communities, and rebuilt skills from the ground up. I learned sales, systems, and strategy. I felt renewed. And through that process, I learned a powerful truth. You are never too old to begin again. You are never too late to dream. Purpose does not follow a timetable.

From that energy came Glluz and Glluztech. They became expressions of reinvention. Proof that experience is not a limitation but an advantage. Proof that creativity does not fade. Innovation, I learned, is not about technology alone. It is about courage. The courage to evolve. To learn. To step forward when others believe your time has passed.

Across every chapter of my life, one simple message has carried me forward. A line from Finding Nemo that holds more wisdom than it first appears.

Keep swimming.
When grief weighs heavy, keep swimming.
When your voice falters, keep swimming.
When you begin again later than planned, keep swimming.
When the future feels uncertain, keep swimming.

Progress is not speed. It is movement.
Persistence becomes transformation.
The future belongs to those who continue.

My parents taught me strength.
My children teach me pride.
My grandchildren teach me hope.
My siblings teach me connection.
My failures teach me wisdom.
My culture teaches me identity.

And my journey has taught me this.

You are given one life. One story. One legacy.

Make it yours.

And no matter what comes next, keep swimming toward the life still waiting for you.

www.ingramcontent.com/pod-product-compliance
Lightning Source LLC
Chambersburg PA
CBHW020156200326
41521CB00006B/397